LIFE

04 SEX

06 PREGNANCY

08 HIV & AIDS

10 DRUGS & THE LAW

13 HEALTH

young citizen's **passport**

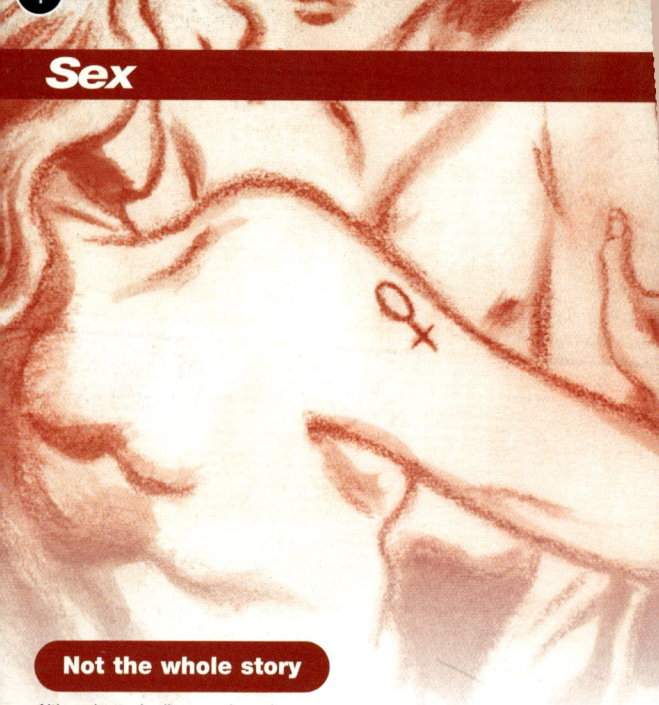

Sex

Not the whole story

Although sex is discussed much more now than it was in the past, most people at some stage in their lives get confused about what they should and should not be doing. Probably the best advice is:

- **don't believe everything you hear,**
- **decide what feels right for you,**
- **talk to your partner and think about their point of view.**

You don't have to do anything that you are not comfortable with and nor should you expect your partner to. There is no golden age by which you should have had sex. Some people will choose not to because they are not interested, or because there hasn't yet been the right opportunity, or because they want to wait until they are married. There's plenty of time and it's OK to opt out!

Pressurising someone into going further than they want, as well as being morally wrong, can reach a stage where it is also against the law. For example, even kissing or touching someone without their agreement can be an assault. In law, both people must agree to what they are doing (known as consent), and they must understand what is happening. The person who gets someone drunk in order to go to bed with them, or takes advantage of their drunken state, risks being charged with rape. (See **Safety**, page 21)

Sex and girls

Age of consent

A girl must be sixteen before she can legally have sex with a boy. If she has

CITIZENSHIP FOUNDATION

ycp

The **Young Citizen's Passport** has been produced by the **Citizenship Foundation**, an independent educational charity which aims to help people become more effective citizens through a better understanding of law and society.

The Citizenship Foundation, 15 St. Swithins Lane London EC4N 8AL

Tel 0171 929 3344
Fax 0171 929 0922

www.citfou.org.uk

Email info@citfou.org.uk

Charity Reg. No. 801360

CITIZENSHIP FOUNDATION

CONTENTS

03 LIFE

17 SAFETY

23 EDUCATION

31 WORK & TRAINING

47 MONEY

59 FAMILY

69 HOME

77 LEISURE

89 TRAVEL & TRANSPORT

101 POLICE & COURTS

111 LAW & GOVERNMENT

119 CONTACTS

young citizen's **passport**

We would particularly like to thank the Service First Unit, the Britannia Building Society and the Law Society for their generous support of this project.

The aim of **Service First - The New Charter Programme** is to improve the delivery of public services and make them more responsive to their users.

At **Britannia** we are committed to remaining an independent, mutual building society, owned by our Members and we share our success with them in the form of our unique Members' Loyalty Bonus Scheme.

The Citizenship Foundation would like to thank the **Law Society** for their continued support with this and other projects.

Editor and main author Tony Thorpe

Concept devised by Andrew Phillips, Chairman of the Citizenship Foundation.

We would particularly like to thank Dan Mace for his help in the preparation of this edition, together with Gill Beasley, Kathleen Bennett, Martyn Bond, Nadia Christodoulou, Liba Cohen, Jonathan Cooper, Mary Domanska, Stuart Duggan, Ceri Edwards, Michael Grimes, Keith Hardy, Ted Huddlestone, Gary Longden, Jan Newton, Jessica Newton, Diane Pearson, Penelope Phillips, Don Rowe, the staff of Doncaster Public Library and to the Bank of England, the Metropolitan Police Service, the House of Commons' Public Information Office, the First Garden City Heritage Museum and Shelter for photographs. Cover photography used with the kind permission of Nick Harthill at Underworld.

and also to Jonathan Bourne, Marie Carmedy, Alex Carruthers, Sarah Cooke, Daniel Jenkins, Hugh Lane, Alison Paton, Kassie Smith, Rosamund Smith, and Rosamund Stock, for their help with the original drafts.

Designed and illustrated by Nomad Graphique; Mike Gibas, Lena Lo, John Dean, Laura Emms, Rupert Boddington and Craig Dixon.

Front cover based on a design by Christopher Goodwin.

Cataloguing in Publication Data

Citizenship Foundation
   Young Citizen's Passport
   I. Title
   344.10287

ISBN   0-340-73051-X

First published 1994
Fourth edition 1999

Impression number	10	9	8	7	6	5	4	3	2
Year	2003	2002	2001	2000	1999				

Copyright © 1999 by the Citizenship Foundation

All rights reserved. No part of this publication may be reproduced or transmitted in any form or by any means, electronic or mechanical, including photocopying, recording, or any information storage and retrieval system, without permission in writing from the publisher or under licence from the Copyright Licensing Agency Limited. Further details of such licences (for reprographic reproduction) may be obtained from the Copyright Licensing Agency Limited, of 90 Tottenham Court Road, London W1P 9HE.

Printed in Spain by Mateu Cromo for Hodder & Stoughton Educational, a division of Hodder Headline Plc, 338 Euston Road, London NW1 3BH.

sex before this, her partner is breaking the law. Girls, unlike boys, cannot be prosecuted for having sex under the age of 16.

The law doesn't usually get involved in punishing girls or women for having sex, although under the *Sexual Offences Act 1956*, a woman who has sex with a boy who is under 16 can be prosecuted for indecent assault, even if he consents.

Sex and boys

Unlawful sex

It is an offence for a boy or a man to have sex with a girl under 16 - even if she agrees.

If the girl is under 13, the maximum penalty is life imprisonment, since a girl of 12 or under is assumed by the law not to understand the consequences of having sex. A man who has sex with a girl aged 13-15 can be given a prison sentence of up to two years. If the man is aged 24 or over he has no defence and will be found guilty. If he is under 24, has never been charged with the same offence and can show he genuinely believed the girl was 16 or over, he may be found not guilty.

Until recently the law assumed that boys under 14 were not capable of having sex and so they could not be prosecuted. Now a boy aged ten or over can be prosecuted for having sex with a girl who is under 13, and it's no defence for the boy to say in court that the girl wanted to have it.

Lesbian and gay relationships

For women

The law says nothing about lesbianism in general - although a woman may be dismissed from the armed forces for being gay.

For men

The age of consent for male gay relationships is 18, although it may be reduced to 16 in the near future.

Under the *Sexual Offences Act 1967*, sexual contact between men is permitted only if both men consent, are 18 or over, and it takes place in private with no one else present. However men, like women, may be dismissed from the armed forces or merchant navy for homosexuality. This regulation is unlikely to change before the year 2000.

For all

There are difficulties for all gay people in a society that doesn't really recognise a person's right to a gay relationship.

If you need to talk to someone who understands, see the **Contacts** list for groups who may be able to help.

Contraception

It is the responsibility of every person who has sex to guard against the risks to both people. It is also important to know how to use the contraceptive properly and how it will affect your body. Good advice is therefore vital. For this you can go to a Family Planning Clinic, your doctor or a Brook Advisory Centre, if there is one in your area.

If you're under 16, a doctor can prescribe contraceptives for you without telling your parents - as long as the doctor believes that you are mature enough to understand what is being proposed. Condoms can easily be bought from supermarkets, garages, chemists, from slot machines in toilets and by mail order. Femidoms, which are a form of sheath for women, are sold in chemists. Both these and condoms are available free from Family Planning Clinics.

Emergency contraception is also available to prevent pregnancy up to 72 hours after unprotected sex or contraceptive failure. Your doctor, Family Planning Clinic or Brook Advisory Clinic can provide further information.

You think yo

Your period is late and you think you might be pregnant. What do you do? To find out if you are expecting a baby, you can ....

● **see your doctor;**
● **buy a pregnancy testing kit from a chemist. These are generally accurate, but some can only be used when your period is at least two weeks late;**
● **take a urine sample to a chemist or health centre for testing. This usually costs about £5, and has the advantage of being quick and, if you wish, anonymous;**
● **visit a Family Planning Clinic or a Brook Advisory Centre.**

What if it's positive?

You will have three choices: to go through with the pregnancy and bring up your child; to give the baby over to be adopted; or to have an abortion and terminate the pregnancy.

None of these may be wholly right - just the best in the circumstances. It is vital that you do everything possible to make the right decision for much hangs upon it, and the consequences can last two lifetimes. So talk, if you can, to your partner in the pregnancy, your parents, good friends and your doctor.

Adoption

Giving up a baby for adoption is not easy - for the mother or father. It's best to talk to someone about this, such as your doctor or someone at the ante-natal clinic, as soon as possible.

The adoption will probably be handled by a social worker who will discuss the kind of family the birth parents want their child to grow up in and will try to find out as much as possible about the birth family to pass

e pregnant?

on to the adopters.

When the child has settled down with the new family, the adoptive parents will apply to the court for an adoption order, which will be granted if the court is satisfied that all is well.

Neither birth parent has the right to see their child after she or he has been adopted, although the child can get in touch with them after the age of 18. Help and advice for anyone thinking of having their child adopted is available through the British Agencies for Adoption and Fostering, see **Contacts**.

Abortion

The question of whether a person should have an abortion obviously has serious moral and practical consequences. Those who are totally opposed to abortion believe that the unborn baby has a right to life in all (or almost all) circumstances. For others however, it is the situation and feelings of the mother that should determine the best course of action. For anyone thinking of having an abortion it is almost always helpful to talk to someone about it. This can be a doctor, staff at the local family planning centre or one of the other centres listed in the **Contacts** section, page 119.

Abortion in England and Wales is legal as long as it follows the law set out in the *Abortion Act 1967*.

This states that an abortion may be legally carried out if:

- two doctors agree that continuing the pregnancy would risk the life of the mother or risk injury to her physical or mental health.
- two doctors agree that there is a substantial risk that the child might be born with a serious physical or mental handicap.

Concern over the mother's mental health is a common reason for doctors to allow an abortion - particularly if they feel she is likely to suffer excessive emotional strain.

An abortion must by law, except in a few extreme cases, be carried out before the twenty fourth week of pregnancy. Anyone wanting to have an abortion using the National Health Service will need to start making the arrangements before the twelfth week.

If you are under 16, your parents must give their consent to end the pregnancy, unless two doctors decide that you are mature enough to understand what the decision really means. Doctors normally insist on having a parent's consent before giving a young person a general anaesthetic.

An abortion can be given without anaesthetic, through tablets. But these are normally used only within the first eight weeks of a pregnancy.

The father, whether he is married to the mother or not, has no right to prevent her from having a legal abortion.

A doctor does not have to carry out an abortion if it is against his or her conscience. If that happens, see another doctor.

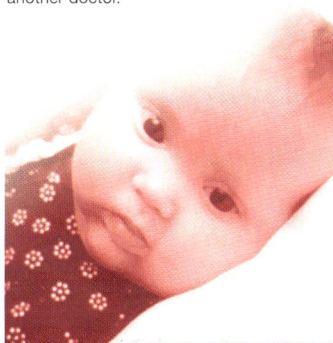

HIV and AIDS

What is HIV?

To understand HIV - standing for human immunodeficiency virus - you have to know something about the immune system which stops us from getting ill.

Blood plays an important part in our body's defence against illness. It contains millions of cells, about 1% of which are white, and a particularly important type of white cell is called the t-helper cell. One of the jobs of these cells is to fight off infection.

HIV is a virus which attacks the t-helper cells. If it grows inside these cells, and other germs get into our body, we have no way of fighting infection. We become ill and develop what is called acquired immune deficiency syndrome, known as AIDS.

At the moment it is not clear whether everyone who is infected by HIV goes on to develop AIDS.

How do you get HIV?

Let's start with how you don't get it. As the virus dies quickly once outside the body, you don't get HIV from
● hugging ● kissing including French kisses ● sharing towels or cutlery ● swimming ● toilet seats ● sharing musical instruments ● giving blood.

The HIV virus is found in the blood, semen or vaginal fluid of a person with HIV or AIDS. Infection takes place when these fluids pass from an infected person into the bloodstream of someone else. This can happen in several ways:

● **by having unprotected sex with someone who already has the HIV virus. This means putting a penis into a vagina or anus without using a condom. The risk of contracting HIV infection through unprotected oral sex is thought to be much lower - but transmission is possible if semen, vaginal fluid**

Sexually transmitted diseases (STD)

Sexually transmitted diseases (also called venereal disease, VD or the clap) are caught from sexual contact with people who have the disease themselves. Most STDs can be cured if treated as soon as possible, and so if you have had sex and you have sores or pain around your sexual organs, see a doctor straightaway. Don't have sex with anyone until it's cleared up, because you will put your partner's health at risk too.

However, not all STDs show signs of infection. Anyone who has sex with someone who is not their regular partner is at risk, particularly if they fail to use a condom. Chlamydia, for

example, can pass undetected for some time, but may eventually produce pain and discomfort, and cause infertility in men and give women problems in conceiving.

Advice and treatment on sexually transmitted diseases is available from clinics dealing with family planning, pregnancy or genito-urinary medicine, as well as family doctors. It is entirely confidential, although if you are under 16, the doctor may be reluctant to do anything without consulting your parents. If this is the case, it is worth checking first whether the doctor is prepared to give advice or treatment in confidence.

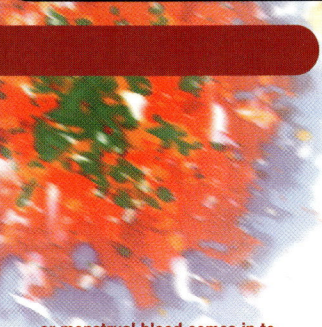

or menstrual blood comes in to contact with bleeding gums or mouth infections. **You can help to protect yourself from HIV infection through sex by using a condom.**

● **by using or sharing a hypodermic needle, which has already been used by someone with HIV, leading to the exchange of a small amount of infected blood.**

● **as a result of a mother with HIV passing it on to her baby whilst it is growing inside her.**

In the past, people have contracted the HIV virus from receiving contaminated blood in a blood transfusion. However, with routine screening of blood, this is not a problem in industrialised countries.

The law is likely to change shortly to make it a criminal offence to intentionally pass on a harmful disease, such as HIV or AIDS.

Anyone who feels they may be at risk of HIV or AIDS should seek medical advice and help, see **Contacts**.

HIV and work

If you have HIV or AIDS, you are under no obligation to tell your employer. However the government advises any health care worker who believes themself to be at risk from infection to seek medical advice immediately. Your employer has a legal duty to treat the information that you are HIV positive as confidential. As a rule, employers are not entitled to tell other workers that an employee is infected with HIV, without his or her permission.

Employers may, if they wish, ask all those who apply for a job to take an HIV test. They cannot insist on existing employees taking a test, unless it is already in their contract. But if you apply for a job and the firm discovers you are HIV positive they are quite within their rights to turn you down. If you lie about it, and they realise you are HIV positive after you have begun work, you may be dismissed.

If you are worried about HIV or AIDS, support and help is available, see **Contacts**.

Prostitution

Prostitutes sell sex for money. They can be either men or women. It is an offence for a prostitute to attract "business" in public (called importuning) and for a man to try to obtain the services of a prostitute from a motor vehicle that he is in, or has just got out of. Prostitutes also risk physical abuse, sexually transmitted diseases, HIV or AIDS and pregnancy.

If the police become aware that a young person under the age of 18 is involved in prostitution, they will almost certainly inform Social Services who will decide whether to apply for an order to take that person into care.

Drugs and the law

Controlled drugs

All drugs produce some kind of change in the way a person's body or mind works, and the availability of most drugs - whether aspirins, alcohol or amphetamines - is controlled by law.

The main law covering the use of dangerous drugs in Britain is the *Misuse of Drugs Act 1971*. Under this Act, drugs which people might misuse have been placed on a list of controlled drugs, and it is an offence to possess, produce or supply anyone with such a drug. The list of controlled drugs is divided into three categories - Classes A, B and C.

Class A drugs

Cocaine, coke, C, or Charlie, is a white powder, sometimes injected, usually snorted through a tube. **Crack** is cocaine treated with chemicals, so it can be smoked. Both give a high, followed by a rapid down. The only way to maintain the high is to keep taking the drug - but regular use leads to sickness, sleeplessness, weight loss and addiction.

Heroin, smack, H or brown is made from the opium poppy - smoked, sniffed or injected. It comes as a white powder when pure. Street heroin is usually brownish white. Heroin slows down the brain and, at first, gives a feeling of total relaxation. Repeated use creates dependency. Overdosing causes unconsciousness and often death - particularly if used with other drugs, such as alcohol.

LSD, also known as acid or trips, is a man-made substance, sold impregnated on blotting paper (often printed with cartoon characters or in colourful patterns) and dissolved on the tongue. It usually takes about an hour to work, and lasts up to 12 hours. The effects depend on the strength of the dose and the user's mood. It generally distorts feelings, vision and hearing, and bad trips lead to depression and panic, or worse, if the user is already anxious.

Ecstasy, known as E, is sold as tablets of different shapes and colour. It makes the user feel friendly and full of energy, and sound and colours can seem much more intense. However the comedown can leave the user tired and low - often for days. Regular users can have problems sleeping, and some women find it makes their periods heavier. Ecstasy affects the body's temperature control and it may cause the user to overheat and dehydrate. There is no guarantee that tablets sold as ecstasy do not contain some other ingredients. This can make their use unpredictable and dangerous.

Magic mushrooms contain hallucinogenic chemicals on the list of controlled drugs. They are not restricted by law when freshly picked, but it is against the law to grow or prepare them in any way, or to possess them with the intention of supplying them to someone else. Most commonly used are the Liberty Cap and Fly Agaric. The effects are similar to a mild dose of LSD, with high blood pressure and possible stomach pains and vomiting. The greatest danger is in eating highly poisonous mushrooms, mistaking them for the hallucinogenic kind.

Class B drugs

Amphetamines, known as speed, billy and whizz and sold as pills or powder, were developed to treat depression. They give a feeling of energy and confidence, but increasing doses are needed to keep up the effect. The downside is anxiety, insomnia, irritability and less resistance to disease and, as with all illegal drugs, there is no guarantee that they do not contain other harmful substances.

Cannabis comes in either a solid, dark lump, known as resin, or as leaves, stalks and seeds called grass. It is usually mixed with tobacco and smoked or (as a resin) eaten. It's called many things, including marijuana, weed, shit, dope, ganja, or hash. It can make the user feel more relaxed and talkative and heightens the senses, especially colour, taste and listening to music. Cannabis can also leave a person tired and moody and make it difficult for them to concentrate and remember things. It also affects co-ordination, making it dangerous to drive or use machinery.

Barbiturates, barbs and blues are used in medicine to help people who cannot sleep. They produce feelings of drowsiness and relief from anxiety. Sold as powder or coloured capsule. Regular use creates dependency. Extremely dangerous when taken with alcohol or other drugs.

Class C drugs

Tranquillisers, known as tranx and benzos are usually taken as pills to reduce worry and tension, but lower alertness affects people who drive or operate machinery. Continued use causes dependency. A number of anabolic steroids are now on the list of controlled drugs after concern over their misuse in sport and body building. They bring many health risks. Supplying such drugs to someone else is now illegal.

The risks

● There is no way of knowing exactly what is in a drug made or obtained illegally. This makes them unpredictable and dangerous.

● All drugs have side effects which may be dangerous and even fatal - particularly if they are mixed or taken regularly.

● Anyone injecting an illegal drug using a shared needle risks becoming infected with hepatitis or HIV, the virus that leads to AIDS.

● Employers and head teachers have a legal duty to confiscate drugs found at work or school and hand them to the police as quickly as possible. Illegal drug taking places a person's job, school or college place at risk.

● A person prosecuted for illegal drug use will not necessarily be sent to prison, but could end up with a criminal record. However a prison sentence is a strong possibility for someone found guilty of supply.

Drugs and the law

Possession

Possession of a controlled drug is an offence, even if it's only a tiny amount. It is not an offence, however, if someone puts an illegal drug in your pocket and you can show it was there without your knowledge - although this will be difficult to prove to a court. In a recent case, someone who put some cannabis in his wallet and then claimed he had forgotten about it, was still found guilty of possession.

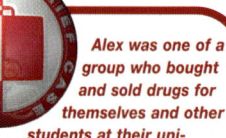

Alex was one of a group who bought and sold drugs for themselves and other students at their university. One day his friend, Paul, took an overdose of heroin and died. It was Alex who had supplied the drug. A court sentenced him to five years in prison.

Supply

It is an offence under the *Misuse of Drugs Act 1971* to supply or to offer to supply someone with a controlled drug. Obviously this includes the sale of drugs - but it is still an offence even if money does not change hands. *Giving* a controlled drug to a friend or *sharing* a drug at a party by passing it from one person to another is still seen in law as supply. (See **Leisure**, page 83)

It is also an offence if the substance sold is not actually a controlled drug, but the seller claimed or believed it to be one.

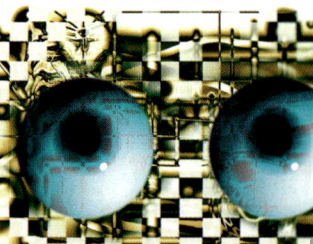

Dennis bought 1000 tabs of what he thought was LSD, and was caught by the police trying to sell them. When the tablets were analysed they were found not to contain LSD, but a harmless vegetable product that was not at all illegal. Despite this, Dennis was accused and found guilty of supplying an illegal or controlled drug, because his intention was to supply LSD.

Production

It is an offence under the *Misuse of Drugs Act 1971* to produce any controlled drug. This includes letting someone use your kitchen or a room for this purpose.

Growing cannabis comes under this heading, and is an offence. Unless, that is, the person can convince the court they didn't realise it was a cannabis plant, and can't tell the difference between that and a geranium.

Police powers

If a police officer has *reasonable grounds* to suspect that someone is in possession of a controlled drug, the officer can search that person and their vehicle and seize anything which seems to be evidence of an offence.

CITIZENSHIP FOUNDATION

Glue sniffing

The effect of solvent abuse is rather like getting drunk on alcohol. However, it takes effect more quickly as the substances enter the bloodstream through the lungs rather than the stomach. Sniffers may experience hallucinations and, if plastic bags are used, may become unconscious or choke on their own vomit. Although potentially very damaging to health, glue sniffing is not against the law, but it is an offence, under the *Intoxicating Substances (Supply) Act 1985* to supply a solvent to a young person under 18 if there is reasonable cause to believe that the fumes might be inhaled.

Tobacco and alcohol

Tobacco should not be sold by law to anyone who seems to be under the age of 16. Under the *Children and Young Persons (Protection from Tobacco) Act 1991*, shopkeepers can be fined up to £2,500 for selling tobacco or cigarettes to under age children. Police officers and uniformed park keepers have, in law, powers to confiscate smoking materials from anyone under 16 smoking in a public place. There has been some discussion about raising the age limit for tobacco sales to 18, but there are, as yet, no firm proposals to change the law.

For details of the law and alcohol, see **Leisure**, pages 78.

Information

Free publications on all drugs and solvents are available from most libraries. The National Drugs Helpline is open 24 hours a day, every day of the year, tel (free) 0800 77 66 00.

Health

Doctors

Confidentiality

Once you're 16, you can decide about your own health care - although, strictly speaking, doctors don't need to consult parents of patients who are under 16, as long as they believe the patient fully understands what is being proposed. Patients also have a right of confidentiality. Nothing they say to their doctor should be passed on to anyone else - not even the fact that they made an appointment.

General practitioners

Everyone living in the United Kingdom, including visitors from overseas, is entitled to register with a GP. A list of local doctors is available from your local Health Authority, Community Health Council (under "C" in the phone book), main post office, library and Citizens Advice Bureau.

You have the right to change your GP at any time. You don't have to explain your reasons for doing so or tell the doctor concerned. However, a doctor does not *have* to accept you as a patient either. If you are refused in this way, the local Health Authority has a duty to give you details of local GPs within two working days. New patients are entitled to a health examination when they join a practice. If you are staying for up to three months in another part of the United Kingdom, you can ask to be registered with another GP on a temporary basis.But if you are leaving home and going to college or university it's probably better to register with a new doctor in the town or city where you are staying.

➤

Health

Doctors

In this way you are guaranteed all the services of the practice if you ever need them. It's helpful to provide your medical card or National Health number when you register. If you don't have these, you will need to know your place of birth and the name and address of the doctor or practice with which you were previously registered.

Charges and prescriptions

Under the *Road Traffic Act 1988*, GPs and NHS hospitals may charge a fee for emergency treatment following a road accident. The charges are imposed on the person using the vehicle involved in the accident and are usually paid for by their insurance companies.

Prescriptions are free if you:
- **are under 19 and in full-time education;**
- **are pregnant or have had a baby in the last 12 months;**
- **suffer from a chronic illness; or**
- **or your partner receive Income Support, income-based Jobseeker's Allowance, Family Credit or Disability Working Allowance.**

Further details are available from GPs, the Citizens Advice Bureau and booklet HC11, A*re you entitled to help with health costs?*, available from libraries.

Records

Your right to see your health records depends on when they were made and whether they are held on paper or on computer. If they are on computer, the *Data Protection Act 1984* gives you the right to see, or obtain a copy of, any information about you, with an explanation of terms that are not clear. A fee of up to £10 may be charged. If you find the records are incorrect or misleading, you are entitled to apply to have the information altered or removed or to add your own version of events.

The *Access to Health Records Act 1990* gives you a right of access to health records kept on paper produced after 1 November 1991. Those made before that date can be seen if they are held on computer, but if they are handwritten, the decision is up to your doctor. The only reason your doctor can give for not letting you see records stored in your file after 1 November 1991 is that doing so would cause serious mental or physical harm to you or someone else.

Dentists

NHS dentists now operate what is called a *continuing care programme*, requiring patients to attend for a checkup or treat-ment at least once every 15 months. Patients who do not keep in touch with their dentist over this period risk losing their entitlement to NHS care with that dentist. Once a dentist accepts a patient for continuing care, the patient must be provided with all the treatment necessary for dental health, on the NHS.

Before each course of treatment, you will receive a treatment plan, showing the work the dentist intends to carry out and what it will cost. The dentist may offer to treat you privately, but should not place pressure on you by implying that the treatment is not available on the NHS. You do not have to accept the treatment being offered.

If you wish to change dentists your local Community Health Council, Health Authority or Citizens

Advice Bureau can provide you with a list of NHS dentists. The Health Authority should, within five working days, be able to find you a dentist who can give you NHS treatment.

If you need emergency treatment, but are not registered for continuing care, you should contact a local NHS dentist to see if he or she is prepared to accept you on an emergency basis. If they can't, contact your local Health Authority, who should be able to find a dentist prepared to provide treatment.

Charges are made for most dental treatment. But dental treatment is free if you:

● **are under 18 or under 19 and still in full-time education;**
● **are pregnant or have had a baby within a year of starting treatment; or**
● **or your partner receive Income Support, income-based Jobseeker's Allowance, Family Credit or Disability Working Allowance or your name is on a current HC2 charges certificate. If you don't qualify for free dental treatment or help with the cost, you must pay up to 80% of the cost, up to a maximum of £340 (April 1998).**

Dentists can charge a patient who fails to keep an appointment or cancels at very short notice. The level of charge varies from one dentist to another.

Opticians

Eye tests are no longer free to everyone. You will get a free test if you:

● **are under 16 or under 19 and in full-time education;**
● **are partially sighted or need complex lenses; or**
● **or your partner receive Income Support, income-based Jobseeker's Allowance, Family Credit or Disability Working Allowance;**

If you need glasses you may be entitled to help with buying them, particularly if you are unemployed or a student on a low income. Further information is available from opticians, the Citizens Advice Bureau and booklet HC11, *Help with health costs*, available from libraries.

The NHS Information Service

A free confidential service, operating 9.30am - 5.00pm Monday - Friday. It can provide information on a wide variety of health matters, including health care and treatment in your area and what to do if you are not happy with the treatment or service you have been given, tel 0800 66 55 44.

Mental health care

Most people who receive hospital treatment for a mental illness are there through choice, or because they have taken the advice of a doctor or social worker. They are known, in law, as *informal* patients. In a relatively small number of cases, a person will refuse to be examined or treated and they will be admitted to hospital *compulsorily*, under the *Mental Health Act 1983* - in the interests of their own health or safety or for the protection of others. This is often called sectioning.

The application for compulsory detention is normally made by a social worker, supported (except in an emergency) in writing by two doctors. One of the doctors must know the patient personally, and the other must have experience in the treatment of mental illness. The patient's nearest relative must also be consulted. An application for compulsory detention can also be made by the patient's nearest relative.

In an emergency, a person can be admitted to hospital for up to 72 hours on the application of a relative or ➤

Health

social worker, supported by a doctor. The police also have emergency powers to remove someone who is in a public place and appears to be mentally ill and in need of immediate care. This would usually be to a place of safety (ie a hospital) for up to 72 hours. Further information is given in the *Patient's Charter - Mental Heath Services* available from libraries and the NHS Information Service.

Voluntary patients can leave hospital whenever they wish, unless the doctor feels this would be a mistake and applies for a detention order. The procedure for releasing patients detained compulsorily is more complex. Your local regional office of the mental health charity, MIND can give you further information. The NHS Information Service, tel 0800 66 55 44, can give you the address & telephone number.

The Patient's Charter

This sets out the standard of service that you should receive from your local hospital, doctor, dentist, optician, chemist and other community health workers. The Charter states that:

● **whatever medical condition you are suffering from, you should not have to wait more than 18 months to be admitted to hospital for treatment. For some conditions, the waiting period should be shorter.**
● **operations should not be cancelled on the day a patient is due to go into hospital or after they have been admitted. If this does happen, the patient should expect to be given a new date for the operation which will be within one month of the cancellation.**

Complaints The *Patient's Charter* also explains what to do if you have a complaint about the NHS, and how your complaint should be dealt with. Details of this kind are also given in

leaflets issued by many GPs, dentists and opticians.

If you have a complaint about your treatment, it's important to make it as soon as possible. Generally, six months is allowed from the date of the incident or the discovery of the problem, as long as it is within 12 months of the initial event.

Copies of the *Patient's Charter* are available from your local library, council offices, the NHS Information Service, tel 0800 66 55 44, and the Welsh Office, tel 01222 823219.

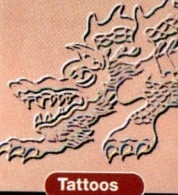

Tattoos

It's illegal for a person to be given a tattoo if they are under 18.

The right to die

The law states that a doctor may give a patient a painkilling drug, which shortens their life, as long as the intention is to relieve pain and suffering and not to kill. If the drug is given with the intention of ending that person's life, the doctor can face a charge of murder.

It is possible to make what is called a *living will* (known in law as an *advance directive*) setting out how you would like to be treated if you ever lose the capacity to make or convey a decision. You must clearly understand what you are doing when you give the directive and, if is done properly, it is legally binding on the doctor. But an advance directive cannot authorise a doctor to do anything unlawful.

Wills Anyone aged 18 or over can make a will, provided they are capable of understanding what they are doing. There is no lower age limit for people in the forces on active service, or sailors at sea.

Blood

There's no legal minimum age to become a blood donor, but the National Blood Service won't accept anyone under 17. Donors usually give about $3/4$ pint twice a year.

SAFETY

18 VIOLENT CRIME

20 HARASSMENT

21 SEXUAL ASSAULT

22 KEEPING SAFE

Violent crime

Although some terrible things do happen, our fear of crime is sometimes greater than it need be. As a rough guide, England and Wales stand about half way down the league of industrial nations for crimes of violence.

Fighting back or getting out

If you're threatened or hit, it's usually better to try to avoid a fight by talking to your attacker or backing off calmly.

If you can't do this, and have to face your attacker, the law says that you can use *reasonable* force to defend yourself. This means that you're entitled to fight back, but not to go over the top and beat up the other person. If you do - you will have also committed an offence.

There is no law which says that you *must* report a crime to the police - but if those responsible are to be dealt with by the courts, then calling the police is just about the only way of doing this. As a victim you may be entitled to compensation for your injuries (see below) but, in order to claim this, the crime must first have been reported to the police.

Arrest - doing it yourself

If you see someone committing a serious offence or have reasonable grounds for believing that they have committed one, you can make a citizen's arrest. But, take care! People have been hurt and even killed trying to do their civic duty. The best advice is to take in as much as you can about the incident, and then to ring the police. If you do get involved, remember that an ordinary person only has the power to make an arrest for a serious offence - such as theft, *serious* assault, or burglary. Don't arrest someone for parking on a double yellow line - unless you want to end up in court yourself.

Neighbourhood patrols also come up against this problem. They can't arrest someone who they think is *about* to commit an offence (it must already have been done), nor can they use excessive force - otherwise they can face charges of assault and wrongful arrest.

Raj ran an off-licence, and had twice been the victim of armed robbery. One night, a man holding a long knife came into the shop demanding money from the till. As Raj was being held with a knife to his throat, his brother came through from the back and the robber ran off. Raj was so angry that he got into his van and chased the man down the street knocking him down and killing him. Raj was found guilty of manslaughter and sentenced to two and a half years imprisonment. The Court decided that he could not have been acting in self-defence because he was, by that time, not being attacked or threatened.

Victims of violent crime

Victims of violent crime can apply to the *Criminal Injuries Compensation Authority* for compensation for their injuries - which must be serious enough to receive an award. The crime must be reported to the police, and an application for compensation made within two years of the incident that caused your injury. It is important to do this as soon as possible, otherwise the claim may be turned down on the grounds that the victim did not do as much as they could to help the police catch the person responsible. However, all cases are treated individually and an exception can be made if, for example, the delay was caused by the after effects of the crime.

Victim Support can give help and advice to victims of crime. Their number is in the local phone book. They also run a helpline, see **Contacts** for details.

If you are a victim of crime and called to court as a witness, you can arrange to see a courtroom before the case starts, have a seat reserved for someone accompanying you and ask to wait separately from other people involved in the case. Details of this and other help available are given in the *Victim's Charter* and the *Courts' Charter*. See **Contacts**.

The words they use

Assault & battery

The word assault is not used in law in quite the same way as in everyday speech. Strictly speaking, an assault takes place when someone causes a person to fear that they are about to suffer immediate unlawful physical violence. Battery is the act of actually hitting that person or using force on them without their consent. Normally assault and battery take place at the same time. But it is possible to be assaulted without battery (raising an arm and shouting threats without hitting anyone), and to be battered without assault (hitting someone from behind without warning).

Burglary

Burglary takes place when a person enters a building without permission, intending to steal, cause unlawful damage, seriously harm or rape someone. Even if nothing is taken or done, a crime has still been committed. It's enough in law to prove that the person intended to break the law in this way.

Robbery

Stealing something with the use or threat of force.

Theft

There are, in law, three parts to theft. A person is guilty of theft who (i) dishonestly takes something, which (ii) belongs to someone else, and (iii) intends to deprive that person of it permanently.

Harassment

Under the *Criminal Justice and Public Order Act 1994*, it is an offence to use abusive or insulting words or behaviour in public in a way that is intended to cause a person harassment, alarm or distress. It's also an offence to put up a sign or a poster that is threatening or abusive in the same way. The law is designed to protect anyone who is being treated like this because, for example, of their race, disability or sexuality. Harassment of this kind is a crime - just like any other - and can be reported to the police, who have a duty to investigate and to try to find those responsible. Statements from witnesses will strengthen a case.

Punishment for offences that can be shown to be racially aggravated, such as harassment, assault and criminal damage now carry increased penalties under the *Crime and Disorder Act 1998*. Local councils also have a number of powers they can use to help tenants or homeowners in their area who are being racially harassed or attacked. They can prosecute residents for harassing or causing nuisance to other residents, they can get a court order stopping people committing certain types of anti-social behaviour, or, if those responsible are council tenants, they can evict them from their home.

The police or local authority can also apply for an anti-social behaviour order. The *Protection from Harassment Act 1997* was passed by Parliament after a number of cases involving men trailing or following women over a considerable period of time. The change in law means that it is now an offence for someone to behave in a way which they know (or ought to know) amounts to harassment or puts a person in fear of violence being used against them. For an offence to be committed, the behaviour or conduct must take place on at least two occasions and is punishable by a period of imprisonment and/or a fine.

Stalking

Somone who feels they might be a victim of harassment can apply to a court, for what is known as an *injunction*, ordering the person committing the offence to keep a certain distance from the victim's house or place of work. The victim can also apply for compensation for the worry they have suffered or for loss of earnings through time off work.

> *Marcia and her 10 year old son were not the only black people on their estate, but for some reason faced almost continuous trouble from one particular group of boys. Marcia first tried ignoring the problem and then spoke to the boys and tried to talk to their parents. Nothing worked. Eventually she complained to the council who investigated the case and obtained a court order requiring the parents of one of the boys to leave their house, which they rented from the council. The boy's parents appealed, saying it was not their offensive behaviour but that of their son. The appeal was dismissed. The judge said that Marcia and her son should not be deprived of their rights just because the parents could not control their son.*

What if it happens to me?

It all depends on the situation. If it's

an isolated incident and the person is someone you don't know, then it may be best to try and ignore it. If you react and get abusive yourself, you run the risk of finding yourself in a far worse situation.

However, if it's happened before, or you're being harassed where you live, then it's important to tell the police - for your own safety. If you are getting abuse at school, college or at work, try and sort it out with the people concerned, but if that's not possible, or successful, raise it with someone in authority. See also the section on **discrimination at work**, page 41.

Someone suffering serious abuse or harassment may be able to claim compensation from the *Criminal Injuries Compensation Authority*, see **Contacts**.

Indecent assault

Under the *Sexual Offences Act 1956*, it is an offence to touch or threaten a person in an indecent way. Groping and unwanted fondling can come into this category. Indecent assault carries a punishment of up to ten years' imprisonment.

Rape A male, over the age of 10, who has either vaginal or anal intercourse with someone who doesn't want him to and who knows that this person is not consenting, or takes no care as to whether she or he does, commits the crime of rape. It's also an offence under the *Sexual Offences Act 1956* to threaten or force a person to have sex against their will, or to give them drugs in the hope that they will give in.

Going out with someone is not, in law, a free invitation to have sexual intercourse with them. Forcing another person to have sex is rape, and it's no defence for the man to say that he was drunk.

It's also rape if the victim was too far gone through alcohol or other drugs to know what they were doing. A wife doesn't have to have sex with her husband. If she does not consent, it's rape (see page 113).

What do you do if you are raped?

Every unwelcome advance is a painful experience. Although you may not want

Sexual assault

to tell anyone, most police stations now have women officers who have been trained to deal with victims of sexual offences in a sensitive way. If you are a woman, you can ask to be examined by a female doctor, and you can take along your parents or a friend.

The police will be able to gather evidence more easily if you report the rape or assault as soon as possible. Reporting the crime early also makes your evidence more believable in Court.

Once a victim tells the police that they have been raped or sexually assaulted, or the suspect has been charged, the victim has the right in law to remain anonymous. Neither their name and address nor their picture can appear in a paper or on radio or TV. Attempted rape is dealt with in the same way.

Help is also available from *Victim Support* and the local *Rape Crisis Centre*, who will talk to any girl or woman who has suffered an unpleasant sexual experience. *Survivors* offer an advice service for men. See Contacts for details. Victims of rape can apply for compensation to the *Criminal Injuries Compensation Authority*. See Contacts.

Male victims of rape are treated in law in the same way as female victims.

Accused of rape?

If you are accused of raping someone, immediately contact a solicitor. Rape is a serious crime, and the punishment can be severe.

Keeping safe

There are some simple, common sense ways to make yourself safer.

- **If you go out - especially at night - tell someone where you are going. If possible stay away from known danger spots.**
- **If you're out late get a lift back, if you can, with someone you trust, or book a taxi, see page 82.**
- **If you walk home, try to get someone to go with you.**
- **Check on the security of your home. Ordinary bolts and chains are not expensive. Advice and information is available from the police, community centres and libraries.**
- **Knowing some self-defence can give you a feeling of greater confidence. The police can give you details of local courses.**
- **If you carry a screech alarm keep it ready in your hand, not in your pocket or handbag.**
- **Men can help by taking care not to frighten women. For example, if you're walking in the same direction as a woman at night, don't walk behind her, cross over the road and walk on the other side.**

questions are all against the law, and carry a sentence of up to six months in prison and a fine of up to £5,000.

If you get such a call, try not to react and don't start talking to the caller. Remember you're in control. Don't hang up, but put the receiver down and walk away for a few minutes. Try to do something else, and then put the handset back without checking if the caller is still there. If the phone rings again, pick up the receiver and don't say anything - a genuine caller will speak first.

If the calls carry on, you can report it to BT and the police. It's very easy to trace calls today, and BT run a free helpline on 0800 666 700. By dialling 1471, you can usually obtain the number of the phone from which you have just been called.

Abusive telephone calls

It is an offence under the *Telecommunications Act 1984* to make threatening phone calls. Heavy breathing, rude words and intimate

Self defence

If you carry something to use for self defence, you run the risk of actually breaking the law yourself. Under the Prevention of Crime Act 1953, it is an offence to carry something made or adapted to be used to cause injury to someone. This includes things like a knife, bicycle chain or a sharpened comb.

Knives

Under the Criminal Justice Act 1988 and the Offensive Weapons Act 1996, it is an offence to have anything with a blade or sharp point in a public place. Folded pocket knives are allowed as long as the blade is less than 3" long. Schools are specifically mentioned as places where articles with blades or points must not be carried, and the police now have the power to enter and search school premises if they have a good reason to believe that an offence of this kind has been committed.

CONTACTS See PAGES 119-127 for organisations able to give help & advice

EDUCATION

24 ATTENDANCE

26 RULES & REGULATIONS

28 EXCLUSION

29 REPORTS & RECORDS

30 EXAMINATIONS

30 BULLYING

young citizen's **passport**

Attendance

Parents have the main responsibility, in law, for their child's education. Under the *Education Act 1996*, it is the duty of parents with children of compulsory school age, to make sure that their child has 'an efficient full-time education suitable to his age, ability and aptitude...by regular attendance at school or otherwise.'

The word 'otherwise' is important here because it allows parents to educate their children at home, and not at school, as long as the arrangements that they make meet with the approval of the local education authority.

Pupils or students?

The word 'pupil' is now defined in law as anyone under 19 years of age for whom education is being provided at school. Students are in further or higher education.

Which school?

Under the *Education Act 1980*, parents can choose the school they would like their child to attend, and the local education authority must follow this wish, if possible. But parents may be refused their choice if the school is full or is some distance from where they live, or it is a church school.

If admission to a particular school is refused, parents (but not pupils) have a right of appeal against the decision and should be told how to go about this in the letter of refusal.

Parents who cannot agree between themselves on a choice of school can ask a court to decide where their child will be educated. In this situation, the court must listen to and respect the wishes of the child concerned.

After their divorce, Peter's parents couldn't agree about where he should go to school. His mother wanted him to attend a boarding school, his father (with whom Peter lived), said that he couldn't afford the fees and felt Peter should go to a day school. Peter's mother asked a court to decide on her son's future education.

After hearing from both parents, the judge decided that Peter's father could well afford the school fees and so Peter should go to the boarding school. However his father appealed against this, saying that no one in court had asked Peter what he wanted. The Court of Appeal did just this. Peter, who was 14, told the Court that he wanted to live with his father and couldn't do so if he was at boarding school. The Court of Appeal felt that it was important to take into account Peter's wishes, and said he could go to the school of his choice.

Costs

State education is free and it is unlawful for schools to try to make parents pay for books or equipment that pupils need for subjects or activities taken in school hours as part of the National Curriculum.
However, charges may be made for.....

● **individual music tuition;**
● **materials for practical subjects (if the pupil wants to keep the finished product);**
● **optional trips taken outside school hours;**
● **board and lodging on school trips, even if the activity is part of the school timetable. Parents who receive Disability Working Allowance, Family Credit, Income Support or income based Jobseeker's Allowance need not pay any of the cost.**

The local education authority has a duty to provide pupils with free school buses or passes if their school is more than three miles walking distance from home. But this does not apply when the child has been offered a place in a suitable school which is closer, which the parents have turned down.
Pupils at school, below the age of 19, are entitled to free school meals if their parents receive Income Support or income based Jobseeker's Allowance. Pupils who bring a packed lunch, must be provided with somewhere comfortable to eat it.

Leaving school or staying on

Under the *Education Act 1996*, compulsory school age begins in the first term after a child's fifth birthday. It ends on the last Friday in June of the school year in which they are sixteen.

Once you pass compulsory school age, your parents cannot force you to stay on at school against your wishes.
It is now the duty of the Further Education Funding Council to make sure that there are enough full-time courses for 16-18 year olds. If your school or college can't offer the courses that you want, you should be offered a place elsewhere.
Students over 16 in full-time education whose parents are on a low income may be able to get an education maintenance allowance or an award from their local education authority. Details are available from your local education office.

Truancy

Parents have a legal duty to make sure that their child attends school regularly or is suitably educated elsewhere. If they fail to do this, they may be committing a criminal offence - and it is no defence for them to say that they didn't know their child was truanting or that they could do nothing to force him or her to attend.

The local authority may also decide to apply to a court for either a supervision order or care order. Under a supervision order an educational welfare officer works with the family to try to make sure that the child is properly educated. A care order is more drastic and may mean the child living in a children's home, from where they will be escorted to school everyday.

Under the Crime and Disorder Act 1998, a police officer who finds a child in a public place, may take that child back to school if the officer believes the child is of school age and is absent from school without permission.

Religious worship & education

The *Education Act 1996* requires all pupils in state schools to take part each day in an act of collective worship which should be wholly or broadly Christian in nature. Parents can ask for their child to be excused. It is also possible for schools to apply to provide worship on a non-Christian basis.

The law states that all pupils (including those between 16-18) should receive religious education as part of their curriculum. Again, parents may withdraw their child from these lessons and make alternative arrangements, but this must not interfere with the attendance of the pupil at school. Pupils cannot opt out of religious education or worship themselves, it must be done by their parents.

Sex education

The law states that all secondary schools must provide sex education for their pupils and in a way that recognises the moral issues involved. However, since the *Education Act 1993*, parents have the right to withdraw their child from any parts of a sex education programme that are not included in the National Curriculum. This even applies to pupils over 16, who can lawfully have sex and marry.

Schools are quite free to discuss questions of homosexuality with pupils as long as it is done in a way (as it says in the *Education Act 1986*), that has 'due regard to moral considerations and the values of family life'.

Government guidelines for teachers state that if they are asked for advice

CITIZENSHIP
FOUNDATION

Rules and regulations

by a pupil, who is under 16, about a sexual matter, they should encourage the pupil to talk to their parents or seek help from a doctor or other health professional. If the teacher believes that the pupil is in physical or moral danger, the teacher is advised to explain the implications of this to the pupil and then to inform the head, who will take what they believe is the best course of action.

School rules

Teachers are entitled to impose punishments - but these must be reasonable.

The *Education Act 1997* allows a school to keep a pupil under 18 in detention after school even though the pupil's parents may not agree. However, the detention must be reasonable in the circumstances and the pupil's parents must have been given at least 24 hours notice of the detention in writing.

Pupils should not be held in detention for too long, nor should their safety be put at risk, eg if, as a consequence, they miss the last bus home.

From September 1999 all state funded schools will require parents (and possibly pupils) to sign a home-school agreement explaining the responsibilites of teachers, parents and pupils.

School uniform

Schools are entitled to insist that pupils wear a particular uniform, as long as it is reasonable and does not discriminate on grounds of sex or race. Parents of pupils who are repeatedly sent home for failing to wear the correct uniform may be prosecuted for failing to ensure their child regularly attends school.

Confiscation

Teachers may confiscate any forbidden items, such as personal stereos, jewellery etc., which they should keep safe and return to the pupil at the end of the day.

In circumstances where illegal drugs or weapons are found, teachers must confiscate the items and hand them over to the police.

Corporal punishment

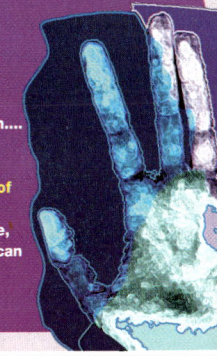

Since 1987, corporal punishment has been banned in every state school in Britain and almost all private schools. (See also page 114.) But under the *Education Act 1996*, there are certain circumstances when a member of staff can use reasonable force to prevent a pupil from....

● committing an offence;
● injuring someone or damaging property; or
● behaving in a way which threatens the good order of the school.

However, if a teacher goes beyond what is reasonable, he or she may be have committed an assault, which can give rise to both criminal charges and a civil claim for damages.

Drugs in school

Schools are encouraged to make clear what action they will take if pupils are found to be using, possessing or supplying illegal drugs in school.

Pupils can be excluded from school on a fixed term or permanent basis, but this should not be automatic, even though using or possessing drugs etc. is a criminal offence. Government guidelines encourage schools to deal with cases individually and to take into account the circumstances surrounding each incident. Although, in most cases, it may be important to tell parents of their child's involvement with illegal drugs, schools are not legally required to do so.

Schools do not have to act on rumours that a pupil is taking drugs in or out of school, but headteachers are expected to inform the police when illegal drugs are found on a pupil or on school premises. A teacher cannot guarantee confidentiality for a pupil who might privately explain that he or she is taking drugs.

Exclusion

A pupil who breaks an important school rule or commits a criminal offence can be excluded from school either for a fixed period of time or permanently. However, Government guidance to schools says that this should only be taken as a last resort. Truancy, lateness, forgetting homework, or pregnancy are not reasons for exclusion. Nor should someone who breaks the law *automatically* be excluded. All pupils should be treated in the same way and all cultures valued equally.

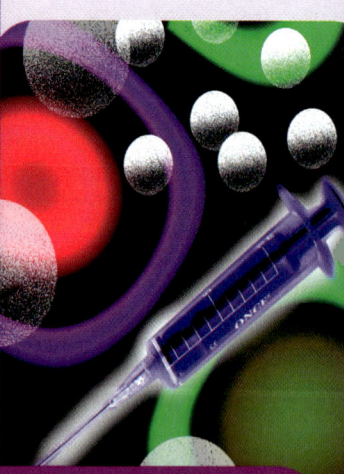

The law allows a teacher to search a student's locker or desk, if it is suspected that it contains illegal drugs (or any other unlawful items). A pupil who is believed to be in possession of illegal drugs can be asked to empty their pockets. If they refuse, the police should be called to deal with the situation. A teacher should never carry out an intimate search.

If a headteacher decides to call the police, efforts must be made to contact the pupil's parents. A young person under 17 should not be interviewed by the police without a parent, adult friend or social worker being present.

Reports & records

A fixed period exclusion is for a set length of time and this may not be for more than 45 school days in a school year.

When a pupil is excluded from school, their parents must be told without delay, and should receive a letter from the head explaining the reasons for the exclusion and for how long it will last. The headteacher should also tell parents of their right to speak or write on behalf of their child to the school governors or the local education authority which, in certain circumstances, has the power to instruct the head to allow the child to return to school before the end of the exclusion.

Parents of a pupil excluded permanently have the right to appeal against this decision to an appeal committee, set up either by the local authority or governors, depending on the type of school. It's important to request this as soon as possible - preferably within seven days of the exclusion. Parents are entitled to a copy of their child's education records and the school's discipline policy. The Government's guidelines on exclusion, called Circular 10/94, are very useful in this situation, as is advice from the Advisory Centre for Education. See **Contacts** for details.

Only pupils or students over 18 have a right to be present at, or to be heard by, an appeal committee.

A written report on a student's progress should be sent to parents at least once a year.

Parents and older school pupils have the right to see records made after September 1989. Access depends on age. If you are:

- **under 16, your parents can ask for a copy of your records, but you have no right to see them;**
- **16 or over, both you and your parents are entitled to see them;**
- **18 and over, only you are entitled to see them.**

However, the school can withhold certain items if it feels they might damage your mental or physical health or that of someone else. They are also entitled to withhold references for work, training or university.

Examinations

If a pupil is refused permission to sit a public exam, eg GCSE or A level, his or her parents may appeal to the school governors against this decision. A pupil who has been entered for an exam but fails to sit it without good reason, can be asked to pay the entry fee.

Anyone caught cheating in a public exam is likely to be disqualified, and the examination board may decide not to mark any of the candidate's papers. Candidates disqualified for cheating have a right of appeal to the exam board. It is an offence to impersonate someone in an exam. Both the impersonated and the person being impersonated can be charged.

If a candidate does not do as well as expected in an exam, the school can ask for their paper to be checked, to make sure that the marks have been correctly added up. Schools can also ask for a re-mark if it's felt that a serious mistake might have been made in the way the paper was marked. If they still remain dissatisfied, the school can lodge an appeal with the examining board and then the Independent Appeals Authority for Schools Examinations.

There is very little that can be done for a candidate who does badly in an exam because of poor teaching, or a failure by a teacher to follow the correct procedure - or even the right books. The examining board can only give grades based on the candidate's actual performance, not on what he or she might have achieved in other circumstances. Action through the courts for compensation would be extremely costly with no guarantee of success.

Bullying

The Government recommends that all schools publish their policy on how they deal with bullying. It's important that parents and the school are told of any bullying as soon as possible - in order to minimise suffering and distress for those involved, and to prevent it becoming so serious that the law becomes involved. Schools have a duty to care for their pupils and must act immediately on any evidence of bullying. In serious cases, schools are now involving the police.

> *Ten pupils, who bullied younger children at a school in Doncaster, were found guilty of a total of 39 charges - including blackmail, robbery and assault. The three most prominent members of the gang were sentenced to four, six and eight months in a young offender institution.*

Safety

Teachers take on some of the responsibilities of parents whilst pupils are in their care (known in law as *in loco parentis*). On a school journey, this can apply for 24 hours a day. The standard of supervision required depends on the nature of the activity and the age or capability of the pupils. Where the action of teachers is called into question, the test that courts apply is whether they acted towards the pupils as careful parents would towards their own children.

CONTACTS See PAGES 119-127 for organisations able to give help & advice

WORK & TRAINING

32 PART-TIME WORK

33 TRAINING   36 APPLYING FOR WORK

38 CONTRACTS

40 HEALTH & SAFETY

41 DISCRIMINATION

43 HAVING A BABY

44 TRADE UNIONS

44 WORKING ABROAD

45 LOSING YOUR JOB

Part-time work

At what age?

If you are under 16 you are restricted by law in the work you can do and how long it can be for.

As a general rule, the only kind of work for children under 13 is doing odd jobs for the family or neighbours, or taking part in plays or films etc., where a special licence is required from the local authority.

Anyone who is 13, 14 or 15 years old may not be employed to work before 7am or after 7pm; on any school day during school hours; for more than two hours on a school weekday, or on a Sunday. Various kinds of work are forbidden, including mining, building and work in transport - unless the only other workers in the concern are members of the young person's family.

The law controlling the work of people under 16 can vary from one town or county to another. Under the *Children and Young Persons Act 1933*, each local authority creates its own by-laws stating the terms and conditions for the employment of young people in that area.

These will state, for example, how long someone below school leaving age may work on a Saturday, and will probably require all employers to inform the council of all young people they employ. Although largely ignored, anyone below school leaving age who has a part-time job is generally required to have a medical certificate of fitness for work and an employment card issued by the local council. Copies of the by-laws controlling the employment of young people in your area can be obtained

A boy of 14, working in a factory making beds, suffered severe injuries when his arm was trapped in an unguarded machine. A court fined his employer £1000 for failing to fit a guard to the machine and £200 for employing a child. The employer also paid £438 towards the costs of the case.

from the local library, council or education office. Further information and advice is available from the Low Pay Unit, see **Contacts** for details.

There are few restrictions on the employment of 16 or 17 year olds. However, people under 18 cannot normally work in a bar, unless they work in a restaurant where drinks are served with meals, or are being trained for the licensing trade under a Modern Apprenticeship scheme.

Employment rights

In 1994, senior judges decided that UK laws unfairly discriminated against part-time workers. As a result, many of the rights of those in part-time jobs (even if it's for only a couple of hours per week) are the same as those of people in full-time employment.

If you are in part-time work you...

● are protected by the disability, race and sex discrimination laws, regardless of how many hours you work or how long you have worked for your employer;

● have the right, if you have worked for your employer for one month, to be given notice if asked to leave and, after two months to receive the terms and conditions of your job, in writing;

● are entitled to redundancy pay if you are made redundant and have worked for your employer for at least two years from the age of 18; and

● are entitled to claim for unfair dismissal if you have worked for your employer for at least two years, and feel you have been unfairly sacked.
For more details of employment rights, see the remaining sections of this chapter.

Training

Youth training

A place on a training programme is guaranteed to anyone aged 16 or 17 who is not in full-time education or work. A place is also guaranteed to anyone aged between 18 and 24 who has not received training because of ill health, disability, language problems, pregnancy or through being in prison or in care. No one can remain on youth training after their 25th birthday. There is no residential requirement for youth training. A young homeless person is eligible for a training place in the same way as anyone else in their age group.

The pattern for youth training varies. It can be full or part time and a mixture of on and off the job training.

If you are accepted on a youth training programme you should be given the following information, in writing.....

● **when the programme begins and ends;**
● **a personal training plan and details of the qualifications you will have an opportunity to gain;**
● **your holiday entitlement; and**
● **your level of pay or training allowance.**

You should also be told whether you are being taken on as an employed or non-employed trainee. It's important to know this, as it affects the terms and conditions of your training.

Modern Apprenticeships are work-based three year training programmes, open to 16-19 year olds, leading to NVQ level 3, equivalent to 2 or more A levels.

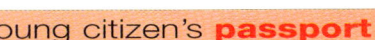

Training

Youth Credits

Everyone in year eleven at school is entitled to receive a Youth Credit to be used to pay for training, including apprenticeships. The scheme operates in different ways in different parts of the country. In some areas, for example, trainees are given a credit card which is swiped as each stage of the training is completed.

Pay

All non-employed trainees receive an allowance of at least £30 a week at the age of 16, rising to £35 when they reach 17. Some training organisations pay more than this, and trainees living away from home may be able to claim extra benefit. Your local Benefits Agency (under *B* in the phone book) can provide more information.

Employed trainees receive a wage that should not be less than the non-employed trainee allowance. They should also receive a pay slip showing wage details before and after deductions.

Help is normally available with the costs of clothing, equipment or tools required for training, and also with travel costs, if they come to more than £4 a week.

Money may be deducted from a trainee's allowance for disciplinary reasons or for unauthorised absences.

Hours & conditions

If you are an employed trainee, you should receive a written statement of the terms and conditions of your work within two months of starting the programme. You should also be given an individual training plan with details

of how your training will be organised. As an employed trainee, you have the same rights as other paid employees.

As a non-employed trainee, you should also receive an individual training plan and details of the hours you are expected to attend. These should not be more than 40 hours per week, plus one meal break each day. If you are asked to stay for longer than this you can refuse.

Holidays and sick leave etc. are decided by your local training agency or TEC. As a trainee, you are entitled to be paid for time off for interviews for work or full-time education, antenatal care, attendance at court and for up to three weeks' compassionate leave.

CITIZENSHIP FOUNDATION

Karen applied for an apprenticeship at a garage in Surrey. She was the best qualified applicant and had already worked in a garage as part of her work experience. At her interview she was asked whether she minded spending all day in a pair of dirty overalls, covered in oil and grease. Karen said she wasn't bothered, but didn't get the job. She took her case to a tribunal where it was decided that she had been unfairly discriminated against. Karen was awarded just over £24,000 for loss of earnings and injury to her feelings.

Equal opportunities

Trainees have the same protection as other workers against unfair discrimination. Help is available at your careers office and the local Citizens Advice Bureau. For more information, see **Equal rights**, page 36 and **Discrimination**, page 41.

Health & safety

Your trainer or employer must make sure that the place where you work is safe, and you have a legal responsibility to follow all safety procedures and use equipment in the way instructed.

If you have an accident, or are worried about safety, speak to your supervisor immediately. If you are injured or become ill while training, you should also contact your local Social Security office. You should continue to receive your training allowance for three weeks after an accident and then you will need to make a claim for Income Support.

Anyone injured on a government funded training scheme may be able to claim *Disablement Benefit* under the *Analagous Industrial Injuries Scheme.* See **Contacts** for details.

Problems

When you start training you should be told what to do if you have any problems while on the programme. If you are unhappy with the training you can discuss it with your supervisor or see the careers officer who may be able to help solve the problem or find you more suitable training.

Non-employed trainees are not entitled to any notice if they are dismissed, nor can they take their case to an industrial tribunal if they feel they have been sacked unfairly. But if they are offered another job, they don't need to work out their notice before leaving. Employed trainees or apprentices receive the same legal protection as other employees and should give whatever period of notice is stated in their contract of employment.

Training

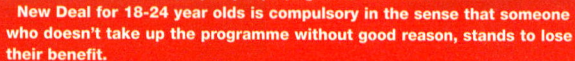

new deal

New Deal takes off

New Deal

This is a new programme designed to help young people into work, with advice, support, training and work experience. It falls into two categories. The first is for people aged 18-24 who have been claiming Jobseeker's Allowance for six months or more. (Some people, such as lone parents, ex-offenders, those who have just left the armed services and those with a health condition or disability need not wait for the six month qualification period.) The second category is for long-term unemployed people, aged 25 and over.

New Deal for 18-24 year olds is compulsory in the sense that someone who doesn't take up the programme without good reason, stands to lose their benefit.

If you are eligible, you will have an appointment with a personal adviser who will explain the programme, give you advice on finding work and monitor progress, based on an action plan that you will be required to draw up. If, at the end of this initial period (up to four months) you are not yet in work, you will be given four options - a job for six months with an employer, work on an environmental project, work in the voluntary sector, or full-time education or training.

Again, if you don't accept any of these alternatives or fail to turn up to interviews without giving a good reason, payment of your Jobseeker's Allowance is put at risk.

If you choose the employment option, you have the same legal rights as other employees - but no right to remain in the post after six months. There is no minimum wage specified for any of the placements but, if it is low, claims may be made for family credit, housing benefit, disability working allowance and council tax benefit. Young people on the environmental or voluntary sector option receive a wage or an allowance equal to the Jobseeker's Allowance, plus £400 spread over six months.

The New Deal Information Line is on 0845 606 2626, open between 8am-8pm, seven days a week.

Applying for work

Equal rights

Most jobs, training schemes and apprenticeships must be open equally to both sexes and to people of all ethnic backgrounds. The laws apply to both full and part-time work, although a few jobs are excluded from the sex discrimination laws. These include acting, modelling and jobs involving physical or close contact with the opposite sex. It is also legal for British firms to discriminate for jobs overseas where local customs frown on certain jobs being done by the opposite sex. There is, at present, no law protecting a person who faces discrimination at work because of their sexuality, although transexuals (people who have changed

CITIZENSHIP FOUNDATION

sex) are protected under UK law from discrimination and harassment at work.

The *Disability Discrimination Act 1995* is designed to protect certain groups of disabled people from unfair discrimination and applies to firms with 20 or more employees. It is against the law to treat a disabled person less favourably than someone without the disability, unless that treatment can be justified for a reason related to the disability. The law, which applies to trainees as well as employees, also states that a firm should make reasonable adjustments to working conditions to allow a disabled person to do their job. If you think you are not being given a fair chance, speak out or write to the firm, giving your point of view. If that gets you nowhere, you can get help from your local careers office or Citizens Advice Bureau. See also the section on **Discrimination**, page 41.

Applications

Read through the application form before starting to fill it in. Draft your longer answers in rough, until you are happy with what you have written.

All the information you give should be correct. An employer is entitled to dismiss someone who deliberately misleads on their application form or at interview.

Your CV

Some adverts for jobs tell you to send for an application form, others will ask for a letter with your curriculum vitae, usually known as a C.V. This is something that you write (or better still type), giving personal details, qualifications, experience and interests. Make several copies and don't forget to keep the original yourself.

Referees

You will need the names of two people who are prepared to act as your referees, to write a short report or reference about you for an employer. One referee is usually your last employer, or the head teacher or year tutor in your school.

Interviews

Arriving late, or not turning up at all, for any kind of interview obviously reduces your chances of getting the job. If you've not been to the office or building before, leave yourself extra time to find it, or better still go round and find out where it is beforehand. If you can't make the appointment, phone or write to explain and ask for a more convenient time.

Have a few questions ready to ask - perhaps about what the course or job involves, requirements and prospects. If they offer you a place or job, before you accept ask yourself if there's anything else you need to know. If there is, ask.

The Jobseeker's Charter

This contains information on what Jobcentres can do to help you find work and the standard of service you can expect. Available from libraries, Benefit Agency offices and Jobcentres.

Contracts

Everyone at work has a contract - whether full or part-time, or on high or low wages.

A contract is another word for the agreement between you and your employer, spelling out the arrangements that will affect your work - such as pay, hours, the sort of job you will do, holidays and the notice you have to give, or you can expect to receive, when your employment comes to an end.

In writing

If you are to be employed for more than one month, you must be given a written statement by your employer, within two months of starting work, setting out the terms and conditions of your job.

This statement should give

● **your job title and place of work;**
● **your starting date;**
● **your rate of pay, and details of how you will be paid;**
● **your hours of work;**
● **your holidays and holiday pay;**
● **arrangements for sick pay and pension;**
● **details of the firm's disciplinary procedures (only if 20 or more people are employed), and how complaints at work are dealt with; and**
● **the amount of notice that you or your employer must give if your contract is to be ended.**

People often think that contracts have to be written down - they don't. They can be agreed verbally - but it's a good idea to have things in writing, in case there's disagreement about what you're expected to do.

Check your contract carefully. Make sure you agree with what it says and that it covers everything you are being asked to do. If it is different from the agreement made at your interview, point this out. Keep safe all pay slips, letters and papers you are given by your employer.

Take care

If you agree to do something on a regular basis which is not written into your contract - like working on a Saturday - you may be, in law, agreeing to a new term or condition of work. If you decide later that working every Saturday is not a good idea, your boss may be entitled to insist that you continue. By turning up for work six days a week, you may have actually changed your contract by your conduct.

Pay

Your wages will either be agreed between you and your boss or else based on rates agreed between employers and the trade union. Either way, your employer must give you a detailed written pay statement each week or month, showing exactly what you are being paid and how much is being taken off in tax and insurance etc.. It is up to your employer to choose how you are paid. This can be by cash, cheque, or straight into your bank account.

Your rate of sick pay must be explained in your contract. It will probably say either that you will be paid at your standard rate for a certain length of time, or that you will be given **statutory sick pay**. This is set each year by the Department of Social Security and is usually at a lower rate than your normal pay. But if you are off sick for four or more days in a row (including Sundays and bank holidays) it means you will receive statutory sick pay from your employer for up to 28 weeks. You don't have to claim statutory sick pay, just follow the rules your employer has for notifying sickness.

You can check what you should receive in leaflets available from social security offices and libraries.

Minimum pay

The *National Minimum Wage Act 1998* sets minimum rates at which people should be paid. It comes into force in April 1999, but does not apply to anyone below

the age of 18. The minimum rates payable to people aged 18-21 will be set at £3.00 per hour, rising to £3.20 in June 2000. For people aged 22 and over, the minimum wage will be £3.60 per hour. At the time of writing, there is some uncertainty whether 21 year olds will move up to the main rate. For more details, phone the Low Pay Unit, see **Contacts**.

Hours

Your hours of work will normally be agreed between you and your employer, although there are some jobs where these are limited by law for reasons of health and safety.

However, in October 1998 the Government put into practice a new European law, known as the *Working Time Directive*, which sets a maximum working week of 48 hours, including overtime. This is to be calculated over what is usually a four month period. It also states the amount of time that nightworkers should be given between shifts and allows them to take free regular health checks.

The Directive does not apply to every type of work and certain jobs are excluded. Workers who believe that the hours they are expected to work do not follow the regulations, can take their case against their employer to an industrial tribunal. For more information contact your trade union or the Low Pay Unit, see **Contacts**.

Holidays

The *Working Time Directive* also gives everyone over 16 the right to at least three weeks' paid holiday a year, increasing to four in November 1999.

Health & safety

Taking care

Employers have a legal duty to take care of the safety of their staff. If they don't, they are breaking the *Health and Safety at Work Act 1974*.

This means that the equipment that you use must not be dangerous or defective, and that the people you work with must work safely and responsibly.

Your duty is to follow safety regulations and to take care of your own and other people's safety.

If you work for a firm where there are five or more employees, your boss must give you details of the health and safety arrangements *in writing*.

It's important to raise the matter - with your supervisor or the health and safety representative - if you are worried about safety at work. If you remain concerned, contact the local offices of the Health and Safety Executive. Your local Citizens Advice Bureau will be able to tell you how to do this.

Using a computer screen

If you have a problem with your eyes that you think might be due to using display screen equipment at work, your employer has a duty to arrange for you to have an eyesight test if you ask for one, and to do whatever they reasonably can at work to reduce further problems. This is all part of a general requirement for employers to check on the health and safety risks to people using computer screens at work, contained in the *Health and Safety (Display Screen Equipment) Regulations 1992*.

Accidents

If you are injured at work, report the matter to your supervisor straightaway and, unless the injury is very small, see a doctor. Make a note of what happened, check to see whether you are entitled to any welfare benefits and get legal advice from either your trade union or a solicitor. You may be entitled to compensation for your injuries.

Gary, 18, worked in a butcher's and was cutting meat when his hand slipped and he cut off the top of two fingers. His boss had often told him to use a special guard - but most people at work ignored this, so Gary didn't bother either. Gary was awarded damages in court because his employer did not make sure that he was working in the right way, but they were reduced by a third because he hadn't followed the safety instructions.

Irene worked as a secretary in an office where several people smoked. Although a nonsmoker herself, she felt no ill effects as the area was well ventilated. However, when Irene's section was moved to another part of the building, with poorer ventilation, the smoke and smell started to become a problem. Despite Irene's complaints, her employer did nothing to discourage people from smoking or to create a better working environment. After nearly three years, Irene left the firm and found another job, but decided to take her case to an industrial tribunal to claim unfair dismissal, saying she had been forced to leave because of her uncomfortable working conditions. The tribunal agreed - an employer has a duty to provide a working environment that is suitable for employees to work in.

Discrimination

It is against the law for an employer to discriminate against someone because of their race, colour, country of origin, nationality, ethnic group, sex or disability. This is explained in four laws - the *Race Relations Act 1976,* the *Equal Pay Act 1970*, the *Sex Discrimination Act 1975* and the *Disability Discrimination Act 1995*.

Not treating a person as well as someone else because of their skin colour, sex etc. is called *direct discrimination*. This is often quite obvious, but can also be more subtle - such as when conditions are laid down for a job that unfairly limit the chances of people from one sex, or a particular ethnic group. This is called *indirect discrimination*.

Help and advice

If you feel you have been a victim of unfair discrimination at work, you can get help from your local Citizens Advice Bureau, Law Centre or trade union. Advice and information on racial matters is also available from the Commission for Racial Equality, and from the Equal Opportunities Commission on sex discrimination.

If you can't sort out things informally, you may be advised to take your complaint to an industrial tribunal, but this must be done within three months (or six months, if it is a claim under the Equal Pay Act). If you win your case, the tribunal can award damages to compensate you for the losses you have suffered. You may be able to settle your case without the need to go to court but, if not, be prepared for a long and difficult battle, and remember to take legal advice.

Discrimination

Eugene suffered constant racist taunts from other workers on the building site where he worked, and the management did little to stop it. They said that "black bastard" and "nigger" were words often used on sites. The tribunal decided that Eugene had been directly discriminated against. He was awarded £2,000 damages.

Susan, a train driver on London Underground, was forced to hand in her notice when new shift rosters meant that it was impossible for her to work and look after her three year old child. She took her case to an industrial tribunal, complaining of sex discrimination. The tribunal decided that the new working arrangements indirectly discriminated against women because more women were single parents.

Unwelcome attention

Sexual harassment covers a whole range of things from rude remarks to leering and unwanted physical contact. They are known in law as *direct discrimination*, under the *Sex Discrimination Act 1975*. Although they usually apply to women, men can be victims too.

If you can, it's often better to try to sort things out personally. But if the harassment continues, don't be afraid to complain. It's not always easy to prove in court, but judges are now prepared to award damages when the victim can show that they have suffered some disadvantage or injury to their feelings from the sexual harassment.

An industrial tribunal decided that a secretary, who was sacked when she complained about being groped by a senior member of staff at a Christmas party, was unfairly dismissed. She was awarded £4,700 in damages.

If you're expecting a baby

Maternity rights

All women at work who are expecting a baby have certain minimum legal rights, see below. Some employers are more generous and provide more than the minimum. You can check your position from your contract. A growing number of firms in Britain offer maternity benefits to men as well as women. But for equal paternity rights for men, move to Sweden or Finland!

Unless they are in the police, work outside Britain, or work as crew on certain kinds of fishing boats, women have the right to....

time off with pay for antenatal care This applies to full and part-time workers, and it makes no difference how long you have worked for your employer. Your employer cannot insist that you make up the time, or that you take the appointment in your free time.

at least 14 weeks maternity leave at least 14 weeks maternity leave. You are entitled to this no matter how long you have worked for your employer, or whether you work full or part-time. Over this period, you still keep all the benefits, apart from wages, that are written in to your contract. This includes holiday entitlement, pension and even a company car, if you have one.

If you've worked for your employer for two years or more, you are entitled to an additional period of maternity absence lasting from the end of maternity leave to the end of the 29th week after your baby is born. You don't receive the benefits that were written into your contract during this time, but you do have the right to return to your previous job or a suitable alternative. You must give your employer at least 21 days notice that you wish to return.

maternity pay If you have been working for your employer for long enough, you are entitled to maternity pay for the time you take off before and after your baby is born. This will probably be lower than your usual rate, unless it says otherwise in your contract. If you are on a low income or have not worked for long enough to qualify for maternity pay, you may still be entitled to a maternity allowance from the Benefits Agency.

A guide to maternity rights is available free from the Department of Trade and Industry, see **Contacts**.

Correct procedures

If you don't follow the correct procedures in applying for maternity leave, you risk losing the right to return to your job after your baby is born. The personnel department at work, your trade union or local Citizens Advice Bureau can explain what you need to do.

Unions

Membership

It is up to you whether you join a trade union. Trade unions don't only negotiate wages for their members. They also give advice, inform members of their rights and act on their behalf over difficulties with their employer. An employer who sacks someone for either belonging or not belonging to a trade union is breaking the law.

Industrial action

If you take industrial action - for example, by stopping work - you may be breaking your contract. If you are, your employer has the right to dismiss you. But it is important that all strikers are treated in the same way. If you are dismissed, and others are not, or if others are taken back on within three months and you are not, you may have a case for unfair dismissal.

This protection only applies to strikes that have been lawfully organised and correctly balloted. You cannot claim unfair dismissal if you are sacked for taking part in an unofficial strike.

If you're sacked or made redundant, your legal rights mainly depend on how long you have been working for the firm.

Notice

Unless you have done something very serious and committed what's known in law as *gross misconduct* - such as theft or fighting - your boss should not sack you on the spot. Your contract should state the notice to which you are entitled, and this usually depends on how long you have been working for your employer.

After one month's employment, either side should give one week's notice. After two years' employment, your employer should give you two weeks' notice, three weeks' after three years, and so on, up to twelve weeks' notice for employment which has lasted twelve years or more.

However, your notice period might be longer if this is stated in your contract, and your employer may decide to pay you instead of letting you work out your notice.

Working abroad

It's much easier to work abroad now than in the past, especially in Europe. Citizens of European Union countries have the right to live and work in any country in the EU, and no longer need a visa or work permit. But entry is not automatic. Your health, lack of money or public security risk can all bar you from admission. Once in a country, however, you should be considered for work in the same way as locals, and you can only be excluded from jobs related to state security and the police.

It's harder to get work in most non-European Union countries, where you will probably need a work permit. This is usually only given on the condition that you already have a job to go to and somewhere to live. It's important to find out everything you need before you leave the UK.

Losing your job

Reasons in writing

If you are fired by an employer for whom you have worked for more than two years, you can ask for a written statement of the reasons for your dismissal. This should be provided by your employer within 14 days.

Unfair dismissal

If you feel that you have been unfairly dismissed, and have worked for your employer continuously for two years or more, you can make a complaint to an industrial tribunal.

If you've not been sacked, but leave your job because of the behaviour of your employer, you may have a claim for unfair dismissal. This is known in law as *constructive dismissal,* but will only be successful if you can show that your employer has broken your employment contract. If you are thinking of resigning because of this, keep a record of what is happening and, before you hand in your notice, write to your employer explaining your reasons for leaving.

Take legal advice before you make a claim for unfair dismissal. Your trade union, local Citizens Advice Bureau or a solicitor can help you. If you are unhappy about your dismissal, don't delay in seeking assistance. **You only have three months in which to make a complaint.**

If the tribunal agrees that your dismissal was unfair, your employer will probably be ordered to pay you a sum in compensation. This is based on the amount of redundancy you would be entitled to, plus a figure for compensation. The maximum basic redundancy award is £6,600 *(April 1998)*, and the maximum figure for compensation is £12,000 *(April 1998)*. It is unusual for a tribunal to order that an employee should be given their old job back.

There are no limits to the damages you can receive if you lose your job through disability, race or sex discrimination.

Losing your job

Redundancy

This happens when an employer no longer needs the job done for which you were employed. Your rights mainly depend on your age and how long you have worked for the firm.

If you are made redundant, you have a right to redundancy pay, if you.....

● **have worked for your employer for a continuous period of at least two years since you were 18;**
● **are under retirement age; and**
● **have not unreasonably turned down an offer of another job from your employer.**

If your employer has gone bust, you may be able to get a redundancy payment from the *Redundancy Payments Service.*

If you are made redundant, get advice from your trade union, Citizens Advice Bureau or a solicitor as soon as possible. If you feel that the way you were chosen for redundancy was unfair or unreasonable, you may be able to claim unfair dismissal. The procedure for this is explained in the previous section.

Information

Your rights to a redundancy payment are explained in the *Redundancy Payments Service Charter,* available free from the Department of Trade and Industry, tel (free) 0500 848 489.

SACKED

Jeannette's son was ill in the night and Jeanette overslept the next morning. When she arrived late at the video rental company where she worked, she was sacked. She explained what had happened, but her boss took no notice. Jeannette took her case to an industrial tribunal, who decided that she had been unfairly dismissed as she had not been given a warning or a second chance.

REDUNDANT

Business was bad and Dean was made redundant from his job at a petrol station. He was given £410 redundancy pay, but soon realised that his job was now being done by the boss's son. Dean hadn't been redundant at all, and so won his claim for unfair dismissal.

We regret to inform you that your services will no longer be needed.
Yours sincerely,

MONEY

48 SPENDING
52 BORROWING
55 BANKS
56 INSURANCE
58 TAX

Spending

Knowing the law

When you buy something from a shop, or pay for a service (like a train fare or haircut) you are making an agreement, known in law as a *contract*.

This means that, in return for the money that you promise to pay, the goods you buy should do everything you can reasonably expect and, in particular, all that the sales assistant and manufacturer claim.

Once a contract has been agreed, neither side can change it on their own. Some shops allow customers to opt out of their contract by agreeing to exchange unwanted items or by providing a refund, as long as goods are returned in mint condition with the receipt. They don't have to do this by law, unless it was promised as part of the contract.

But what about your rights if the goods you have bought are faulty?

The Sale of Goods Act

The law applying to most everyday purchases is the *Sale of Goods Act 1979*. It says that when you buy goods from a shop or trader, but not a private sale (eg through a 'small ad'), they must be ....

 of satisfactory quality This means that they must be free from faults and not scratched or damaged, and equally applies to something you buy in a sale. However, this rule does not apply if the fault was pointed out by the sales assistant or if you inspected the item and had a good opportunity to discover the fault.

Second-hand goods bought from a shop or trader must also be of satisfactory quality - but this protection does not apply if you bought them privately, when the buyer is responsible for the quality of what they decide to buy.

as described The goods must be the same as the description on the packaging, or advertisement or given by the assistant at the time of sale. A bracelet marked solid silver, must be just that. Cosmetics described as being not tested on animals cannot have been the cause of suffering to countless laboratory rabbits and mice.

This rule also applies to second-hand goods, *including* those sold privately.

☑ fit for all their intended purposes This means that they must do what the seller, packaging or advertisements claim. A watch sold as waterproof should not stop if you forget to take it off in the shower.

Getting it right

If you're buying something expensive, it's worth doing some research beforehand. *Which?* magazine, available in most libraries gives a guide to the price and performance of most products. It's also OK to go to a shop and to ask just to see an item, without buying it. If, eventually, you decide to make a purchase, keep the receipt in case you have a complaint.

Service!

Dry cleaners, shoe repairers, mechanics, hairdressers all provide a service - and you are protected by law if that service is inadequate.

Under the *Supply of Goods and Services Act 1982*, a service must be provided...

● **with reasonable care and skill;**
● **within a reasonable time; and**
● **for a reasonable charge.**

Problems are less likely to occur if certain things are agreed before the work is started. How much will it cost? How long will it take? What happens if it can't be mended? Try to sort these out first.

Handle your complaint just as you would were it for faulty goods. Don't be afraid to seek advice. Help is available from your local Citizens Advice Bureau or consumer advice centre.

Some trades, such as travel agents, garages, dry cleaners, shoe sellers etc. have their own associations laying down a code of practice or standards. These have no legal standing, but the associations can put pressure on their members to treat customers' complaints in a reasonable way. It may be worth a try, and your local library can give you the address to contact.

Put downs

Some shops and firms will do as much as they can to help you with a problem over something you have bought, others may claim that there is nothing they can do. Don't give up if the shop tries to get out of its legal obligations.

We'll send it back to the workshop *Only if you want them to.* If the fault appears shortly after you buy the goods and you haven't misused them, you need not face further inconvenience by having them repaired. You are entitled to your money back. But, if the item worked well at first and then developed a fault, you may still entitled to some or all of your money back, to be offered a replacement or to have it repaired free of charge. It all depends on how long you have had the goods, the seriousness of the

fault and whether you can convince the shop that it's not reasonable for a fault to develop so soon.

You'll have to take it up with the manufacturer *Wrong.* You bought the goods from the shop. Your contract was with them, not a factory owner on the other side of the world. If the goods genuinely don't work, the shop has not kept its side of the contract and you have a right to your money back. The shop will have its own claim against its supplier.

We'll give you a credit note *No.* If the goods are faulty, you're entitled to your money back. You don't have to accept a credit note.

Sorry, it's out of guarantee *This can be tricky.* A major problem with an expensive

Finding it's wrong

If you are not satisfied with something that you have bought....

1 Stop using it straightaway and take it back, with the receipt and guarantee (if you have one), to the shop where you bought it. It strengthens your case if you can do this as soon as

possible. Your contract was with the shop, not the manufacturer, so it is the shop's responsibility to deal with your complaint.

2 Before you take the goods back, decide what you are going to say and what you would like the shop to do. Do you want your money back, or will you be happy to exchange the item for one that works?

computer three months after the guarantee has run out means a large repair bill . Raise it with the dealer and ask to talk to the manager. Produce the documentation and use the manufacturer's literature (which probably stresses reliability and quality), to point out that it is not reasonable to expect a failure after such a short period. There's no hard and fast law about what is reasonable in terms of a product failure. It depends on the circumstances.

We don't give refunds on sale goods *Wrong.* Unless the fault was pointed out to you, or was something you should have seen when you bought them, goods bought in sales carry all the protections of the *Sale of Goods Act 1979.*

We'll give you a replacement *Only if that's what you want.* However, if by now the fault has led you to decide that you don't really want the product after all, you are entitled to your money back - not a replacement. It's up to you to choose what to do.

The Small Claims Court

If you cannot get any satisfaction over a problem with faulty goods or poor service, you can write to the person concerned warning them that you will try to recover the money they owe by taking your case to the small claims court (strictly known as the small claims procedure). This is an informal way of settling disputes, at a fraction of the normal cost, in which a judge hears your case in private, without the expense of lawyers. Cases usually involve claims of no more than £3,000 (to be raised to £5,000 from April 1999), and can be brought only by someone of 18 or over. You can get more details from your local county court (under Courts in the phone book), the Citizens Advice Bureau or a consumer advice centre.

3 Think about your legal position. A faulty stop button on a personal stereo means that it is not of satisfactory quality. Don't be afraid to use the law when making your case.

4 Keep calm. If the shop assistant doesn't help, ask for someone more senior.

5 If you bought the goods by mail order or from a shop some distance away, it's easier to telephone or write. Keep a copy of all letters, send a photocopy of your receipt (keep the original), and if you talk on the phone get the name of the person you spoke to. Make a brief note of the conversation.

Borrowing

Loan

A loan is a contract between you and the lender. It is important to know the rate of interest you will be charged on the loan, and to be confident that you will be able to make all the repayments required.

A loan is not usually available to anyone under 18 because in law, as a minor, they cannot be held accountable for their debts. This means that if they did borrow money and failed to keep up with the repayments, it would be difficult for the bank or loan company to get the money back. Anyone under 18 applying for a loan normally needs an adult to act as guarantor.

Overdrafts

An overdraft is an arrangement with a bank, allowing you to borrow up to an agreed maximum. You will only be charged interest on the amount overdrawn, but the rate will be high and the money is repayable when the bank wants, even immediately. Many banks offer free overdrafts to students, see **Banks,** page 55.

Credit

Buying goods on credit allows you to pay for them over a period, or at a later date, but it's usually more expensive than paying by cash because of the interest charged on the credit. This is shown as the APR, which stands for *Annual Percentage Rate,* and shows the full rate of interest paid. Generally, the lower the APR, the better the deal.

Before giving you credit, the lender will need to know whether you are an acceptable risk. The company will check your record with probably one of two credit reference agencies, who have information on almost every adult in Britain. You have a legal right, for a small charge, to see a copy of your file held by an agency. If you have been refused credit and want to know which agency the lender used, you must write to them within 28 days of being turned down. If the information they hold on you is incorrect, you can ask for your file to be changed. For more information contact the Citizens Advice Bureau, a consumer advice centre or the Office of Fair Trading, see **Contacts.**

Store cards

Sometimes called *charge cards,* are available from many High Street stores and allow you to buy goods up to a certain amount, at one particular store or group of shops. You either pay the bill off in full or in fixed monthly payments plus interest on the amount you leave unpaid.

Credit cards

These cards, such as Visa or MasterCard, can be used in many places, both in this country and abroad. Again you have a limit up to which you can spend, but *you* decide how much to pay off each month, as long as it is above a certain minimum. This is usually £5 or a percentage of the total debt, whichever is greater. Interest is not charged if you pay your balance in full at the end of each month. But if you don't, the high interest rates mean that it can be difficult to reduce the size of your debt.

If you are not satisfied with something you bought by credit card and the shop refuses to give you a

refund, you can claim your money back from the credit card company instead. Under the *Consumer Credit Act 1974* the credit card company shares responsibility with the shop for problems with any items that you have bought with the credit card which cost between £100-£30,000. It may be easier to get your money back from the credit card company than the shop - and you don't need to have paid all or even most of the price of the item by credit card, as long as the total price is over £100.

Charge cards

Diners Club and American Express are like credit cards, but customers must pay off the full debt at the end of each month.

Hire purchase

This is typically used for expensive items such as cars, home video systems or computers, where a credit card limit is too low. The sums are worked out when you buy the goods and you are told exactly how much you will have to pay, over what period and what the overall cost will be. All this information must be provided for you by law, to protect you from unexpected interest charges. If you are under 18 or not a homeowner, you may need someone to guarantee the payments in case you are unable to keep them up. Beware of the "small print". If it's not clear, get someone to check it for you.

If you buy something on **hire-purchase**, the shop sells it not to you, but to a finance company. You then hire it back from the finance company for a fixed period of time, at the end of which the company sells it to you for a small sum (hence hire purchase). Only then technically is it yours to do with what you like.

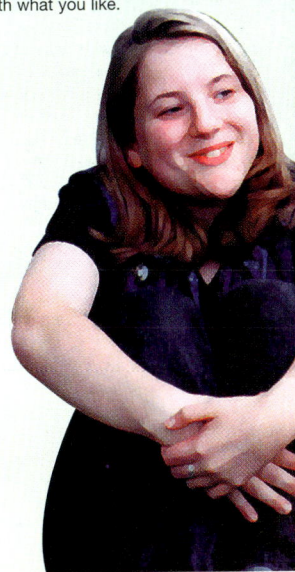

Borrowing

DEBT

CREDIT

final demand

Second thoughts

What do you do if you sign a credit deal and then change your mind? If you signed the credit agreement at *home,* you will receive through the post a second copy of that agreement from the finance company. You have *five days* from the time this arrives to cancel the agreement.

An agreement for credit arranged in the *shop* or other *business premises* is harder to break, unless the form has to be sent away to the finance company for signature. In this case, the contract or agreement will not have been completed, and you will have a short period in which to stop the agreement, if you act quickly.

Never sign an agreement without all the details being filled in and try, if you can, to get a written quotation to take home to study before you agree to anything.

You can't keep up the payments

Contact the lender at once and explain what has happened. You may be able to make smaller monthly payments by extending the period of the loan until you are in a better financial position. Keep copies of all letters you write. If you telephone, ask the name of the person you speak to.

If you have bought the goods on HP and payment is overdue, the finance company must give at least seven days notice before taking action against you. If you have already paid a third or more of the purchase price, the finance company must first obtain a court order before demanding back the goods.

The goods are faulty

Don't stop your payments until you've exhausted all possibilities. If you just can't get anywhere, then stop the payments and, at the same time, write to the finance company explaining what you are doing and why. With luck they will put pressure on the supplier to put matters right.

If you paid for the goods by credit card, and they cost more than £100, the card company also has responsibility for making sure that the goods are of the right quality and standard. This means that if something goes wrong, you can make a claim against the credit card company as well as the supplier, because technically you have bought them from the credit company.

Banks

Many people keep their money in a bank, building society or Post Office account. In fact if you have a job, your employer can *insist* that you have an account to pay your wages into. All have leaflets explaining the services they offer and the different kinds of account that you can choose.

All provide you with a cheque book and cash card for taking cash out of your account, but if you're under 18 it's quite difficult to get a cheque guarantee card which allows you to pay for goods by cheque in a shop. This is because if someone under 18 (legally known as a "minor") goes overdrawn, the bank or building society could find it very difficult to get the money back. Some banks, however will give a cheque guarantee card to 16 or 17 year olds who have an income or can provide someone who will act as a guarantor.

If you go overdrawn, that is spend more money than you have in your account, you will usually have to pay interest and bank charges. It is a criminal offence to write a cheque knowing that you don't have enough money in your account to meet it and that the cheque will take you over your overdraft limit.

If you don't pay tax and have savings in a bank or building society, let them know, otherwise they will take off tax from your interest. For further information, see the section on **Tax**, page 58.

Banks offer all kinds of incentives to get young people to open an account, including interest-free overdrafts. This can be useful if you are a student, as most find it very difficult not to get into debt during their time at college or university.

If you are not happy with the service you receive from a bank, and get no satisfaction from the manager or head office, you can take your complaint to the *Banking Ombudsman*, see **Contacts**.

Cheque books and cards

Cheque guarantee cards enable you to pay for goods by cheque up to the value given on the card - usually £50 or £100. The card is not valid if this limit is exceeded or if more than one cheque is written in payment for the goods.

Banks and building societies advise customers not to keep their cheque book and card together. The bank should be told, as soon as possible, if either the cheque book or card is lost. You are not liable for any debts on cards or cheques used without your permission once you have informed the bank of the loss. If your card is lost or stolen and then used by someone before you have told the bank, you can be required to pay up to £50 of any debts incurred.

Insurance

Insurance is a way of protecting yourself and your property from an unexpected loss or mishap. You can insure yourself against almost anything - losing your possessions in a fire, having them stolen or damaged, or having to face unexpected medical bills on holiday abroad. If you drive a car or motor cycle, you must be insured by law, see **Travel and Transport**, page 95.

In return for a premium - an agreed amount of money you pay each month or year - an insurance company will, if the worst does happen, pay you compensation for the losses or damage that you insured against.

Buying insurance

There are two ways of obtaining insurance. You can either deal directly with the company, or go to a *broker*.

Most large insurance companies have offices in the major towns and cities. Their number is in the Yellow Pages or local phone book. You can often deal directly with them and arrange your insurance cover by phone.

Insurance brokers are agents who can help you choose an insurer and arrange the *policy* for you. They don't usually charge you for this, but instead make their money from the insurance company that you have decided to use.

It's important to think carefully about the kind of cover you want, and to check exactly what the *policy* offers. Look out for things that are not covered in the policy, and check whether you will have to pay the first part of any claim, called an *excess*. Many policies now require you to pay the first £50 of any claim. It's a good idea to obtain free *quotations* from several companies before deciding which one suits you best. Ask the salesperson or insurance broker to explain anything that isn't clear.

All the information you give should be as accurate as possible. Questions must be answered truthfully, and any other information that could be relevant should also be given. If it's not, the insurance policy will be invalid.

Keep a copy of any form that you complete, and when you renew your insurance (usually done each year) don't forget to tell the insurance company about anything that has changed that might affect your insurance position.

The words they use

Broker an agent who can help you choose and apply for insurance.

Cover insurance against loss or damage.

Cover note a temporary document showing that you have insurance cover, usually sent out while the official certificate is being prepared.

Excess the amount you will have to pay towards the cost of your claim.

No claims bonus the discount you are given on your premium if you haven't made a claim.

Policy the document setting out the terms and conditions of your insurance.

Premium the amount you pay for your insurance.

Quotation a statement of the amount you will have to pay for the insurance you asked for.

Tax

Money paid in income tax is used to pay for services provided by the state - such as health, education, defence etc.. Everyone who earns or receives income over a certain amount in a year pays income tax and, generally speaking, the more you earn, the more you pay. As well as earnings from full and part-time work, tips and bonuses, tax is also paid on interest from savings with banks, building societies and some National Savings accounts, on unemployment benefit and on profits from a business and dividends from shares.

Your employer will usually take the tax from your earnings each time you are paid and pass the money on to the tax authorities, called the Inland Revenue. People who are self-employed usually pay tax in a lump sum once or twice a year.

Everyone is entitled to receive a certain amount of money on which they pay no tax at all. This is called a *personal allowance* which, for a single person in 1998/9, is £4,195. Income tax is paid only when your income rises above this. There are other allowances which you may also be able to claim, eg for the cost of tools or special clothing if they are not provided by your employer. If you are on a training programme, your grant in most cases is not taxable.

Part-time workers should not have tax deducted from their pay, unless their income is above £80 a week. If you are a student with a holiday job, ask your employer for a form P38(S) if you think your total taxable income for the year (including earnings and unemployment benefit), will be less than the basic personal allowance, ie £4,195. Fill in the form, return it to your employer, and you should then be paid without tax being deducted.

If you have been working and paying tax, but believe your total income for the year will be less than £4,195, ask for form P50 from your local tax office, and return it completed with your P45 from your employer. The Inland Revenue publishes free booklets on tax, obtainable from your library or nearest tax office (under Inland Revenue in the phone book). *The Taxpayer's Charter* outlines the service you are entitled to expect from staff at the Inland Revenue.

Failure to complete your tax forms correctly can mean extra intersst payments and even fines. The Inland Revenue run a free telephone helpline, charged at local rates, giving information and advice on tax. See **Contacts** for details.

Benefits

You may be entitled to Income Support, Maternity Allowance, a disability allowance or other social security benefits. Benefit rates normally change once a year, in April. Leaflets explaining this are available from Social Security and Benefit Agencies offices, and sometimes local libraries and post offices. A freephone benefits information and advice line for disabled people and their carers is available on 0800 88 22 00

The *Benefits Agency Customer Charter* explains the standard of service that local offices should offer and is available from Benefits Agency offices. See also **Contacts.**

CONTACTS See PAGES 119-127 for organisations able to give help & advice

FAMILY

60 NAMES

61 CITIZENSHIP

62 PARENTS

63 ADOPTION

64 LIVING TOGETHER

66 DIVORCE

young citizen's passport

Names

Within 6 weeks of birth, the birth and name of a child must be registered with the District Registrar of Births, Marriages and Deaths. This is usually where the child was born or where the child will live.

The birth can be registered by either parent if they are married, but only by the mother if they are not. If unmarried parents want both their names to appear on their child's birth certificate, then they must both be present when the child is registered.

Changing your name

Over 18 you can call yourself what you like and, if you want to change your name, you can just go ahead and do it. But you can't change your name to mislead or defraud someone.

Although you are free to be known by whatever name you wish, it can be difficult to *prove* your identity if the name you use is not the same as the one on your birth certificate. The best way to confirm your new name is by a *change of name deed*, which is a statement announcing your new name, witnessed by a solicitor. Your local Citizens Advice Bureau can give you more information on this.

Under 18 A child's name can be changed with the agreement of both parents, unless the child is in care or a ward of court. In this case the child's name cannot be changed without the agreement of the court or everyone with responsibility for the child. The child can also object by applying to court.

If a parent wants to change their child's name, but the other parent or the child objects - then the parent or the child can apply for a court order to prevent this. Courts are very reluctant to agree to change a child's name because of the importance of a name to a child's sense of identity.

If *you* wish to change your name you will need your parent's consent or a court order. If you are over 16 you can change your name by deed and register it at court. If your parents object, you may need a court order to override their objection.

If you marry

Although many women in Britain change their surname when they marry - they don't *have* to. A woman can keep her own family name, or she can make a new one by joining her name with that of her husband.

aljinder

Citizenship

Most of our legal rights and responsibilities arise just because we are living, working, studying etc. in a particular place - in our case, Britain. This is citizenship in its widest sense.

Sometimes, however, people need to know which country they are a citizen of (or what their nationality is). Countries can base their rules on a number of questions, such as where a person was born, how long they have lived in the country and where their parents were born or live.

In brief Anyone born in the United Kingdom before 1 January 1983 is automatically a British citizen. If you were born in the UK on or after this date you are a British citizen by birth if either of your parents are British citizens or they are entitled to live here permanently. If your parents are not married, only your mother's position counts.

Becoming a British citizen by naturalisation or registration depends on a number of different factors, such as if you marry a British citizen, how long you have lived here, if you are permanently settled here (or intend to remain here permanently) and if you are of 'good character'.

This is a complicated area of law. If you have a problem, you will need specialist advice. Your local Citizens Advice Bureau can help you find this.

Parents

How the law works

There are laws which list the exact rights and duties of parents. It would be impossible to write down everything a parent should do for a child.

Instead, the law states that all married parents and unmarried mothers (but not unmarried fathers), automatically have parental responsibility for their children. This means that they have the responsibility and authority to care for the child's physical, moral and emotional needs.

If the child or young person is in care, parental responsibility is shared between the parents and the local authority.

Today the law tries to put the interest of the child first. The powers that parents have to control their children are designed to exist for the benefit of the child, not the parent. Those who deal with children in a legal setting, such as social workers, doctors and lawyers, must take careful note of what a child says, particularly when the child is able to understand all the issues involved. Parental responsibility ends when the child reaches 18. As a very experienced judge once said;" in law, parents begin with a right of control, but by the time the child is eighteen they can do no more than advise."

Providing a home

Parents have a duty to look after and care for their children until they are 18. However, once someone reaches the age of 16 they can normally leave home without their parent's permission. The police and other authorities are unlikely to stop anyone leaving home, even against their parent's wishes, unless they are under 16, in some kind of danger or are unable to look after themselves. For more on this see the section on **Home**, page 71.

Discipline

Parents have the right and duty to discipline their child - and this can include smacking. Parents can also agree to others, such as a child minder, disciplining their child. But corporal punishment must be "moderate and reasonable". If it is too harsh, the child's name may be placed on the child protection register, the parents prosecuted, or the child taken into care for protection. In several other European countries, notably Sweden, Norway, Finland, Denmark, Austria and Cyprus, it is illegal for a parent to strike a child.

Education

Parents have a duty to make sure that their child has a proper full-time education, up to the age of 16. They have a right to choose their child's school (although there is no guarantee that they will get the school of their choice), and can, if they wish, withdraw their child from religious education. (See also pages 26.)

Religion

Parents can decide the religion in which their child will be brought up. If they can't agree between themselves,

Adoption

they can go to court, where a judge will decide what is in the best interests of the child.

A court will probably allow the child to make up his or her own mind, as long as the child clearly understands what is involved. However, the law is not absolutely clear on this.

Medical treatment

Before treating a young person under 16, doctors are advised (where possible) to obtain the parent's permission unless it is an emergency or the young person is clearly able to understand what the treatment involves. Young people of 16 and over can consent to their own medical or dental treatment without referring to their parents.

Baby-sitting

There is no law giving the minimum age for a baby-sitter, nor one stating how old a child must be before it can be left alone. The nearest the law comes to this is in the Children and Young Persons Act 1933 , which states that a child under the age of 12 must not be left alone in a room with an unguarded fire.

Parents have a legal duty to care for their children, and some of that responsibility is passed on to a baby-sitter when the children are in their care. This means that parents must choose a baby-sitter who is able to look after their children properly. If a serious accident occurs while they are out, the parents may have to convince a court that they had done all that they could to make sure their child was being looked after properly. A baby-sitter who was under 16 would probably be thought too young to deal with an emergency.

Ages

Anyone who is under 18, and has never been married, can be adopted. You must be at least 21 to adopt a child.

When children are adopted, they are treated in law almost as if they had been born to the couple or person who adopted them. Parents who adopt children are advised to be open about their child's birth family from the start.

At 18, people who have been adopted have the right to see a copy of their original birth records, and can get more information from the agency that arranged their adoption. For those born before 12 November 1975, counselling to prepare them for this is compulsory (and optional for anyone born after this date).

Further help for adopted people and their birth relatives who wish to get in touch is available through the *Adoption Contact Register* and *NORCAP*. See also **Life**, page 6, and **Contacts**, for further details.

Living together

An increasing number of couples live together, sometimes with the thought of getting married later on, and sometimes not. Although this is a matter of personal choice, the law treats married and unmarried couples very differently.

Money and finance

Couples who marry have a legal duty to look after one another, and to provide each other with financial support. This may continue even if the marriage ends in divorce. But a couple who live together without getting married are under no such duty, unless it is something they have specifically agreed to.

When children are involved, both parents, whether married or unmarried, have a legal responsibility to look after them and provide for them until they have completed full-time education.

Couples who marry receive an extra tax allowance, which means that they usually pay less tax than if they were just living together. Maternity and pension rights are also better for a married than an unmarried woman.

If a married person dies without making a will, their partner is entitled to all or most of their possessions. But if they were not married, it can be very difficult for the partner to obtain any of the deceased's possessions.

Children

Parents who are married share the parental responsibility

in law for their children. This means that both can make decisions about their children's upbringing. Unmarried fathers have this right if the couple have signed a parental responsibility agreement, or if the father has made a successful application to court for parental responsibility.

Home

A married couple have equal rights to occupy their home, whether they rent or own it. This continues even if their marriage fails, unless the court orders otherwise.

When an unmarried couple live together, however, the non-owner of the home may have no right to occupy the property. Couples can avoid difficulties caused by this by using a solicitor to write a formal contract setting out what would happen to their house and contents etc. should the relationship come to an end.

alive). They need not be a churchgoer, but must satisfy the legal requirements and qualify as a resident of the parish. Members of other faiths must, before the religious ceremony, obtain a civil certificate or licence from the senior registrar in the district where they live.

Under the *Marriage Act 1994*, couples can choose to marry in any registry office in England and Wales or in other places that have been registered (such as a hotel or stately home), but not in a temporary structure like a marquee, or in the open air.

Being married to more than one person at the same time - called bigamy - is normally a crime. But the marriage is recognised in England and Wales if it took place in a country which allows marriages of this kind, and if each partner was legally free to marry in that way.

Breaking up

A marriage can be ended only by a court order, and there can be no divorce in the first year of marriage. A couple who live together can end their relationship anytime they choose, without having to go to court.

Marriage

No one can be forced to marry against their wishes, and each partner must be 16 or over and unmarried. A person who wants to marry, but is under 18, needs their parent's written consent. It's a criminal offence if a couple get married without this, but the marriage is still valid. However marriages involving someone of 15 or under, or members of the same sex (even after a sex change operation), are not recognised in law.

Almost anyone can be married in an Anglican church (unless they are divorced and their former partner is still

Engagement

Until the law was changed in 1970, an engagement was seen as a legal agreement or contract between two people to marry. If it was broken, one person could sue the other for damages. If someone breaks off their engagement today, there is usually no legal duty even to return the ring. The engagement ring is seen as a gift, and may be kept, unless it was originally agreed to return it if the marriage did not take place.

Divorce

Grounds for divorce

Under the present law, a person who applies for a divorce must prove to the court that their marriage has irretrievably broken down. They can show this if one of the following five things have happened....

1 the other partner has committed adultery, ie had sexual intercourse with another man or woman;

2 that the other partner has behaved unreasonably. This covers many things, including assault, refusing to have children, being excessively dirty or unsociable;

3 that they have lived apart for 2 years, and they both want a divorce;

4 that they have lived apart for 5 years and only one partner wants a divorce; or

5 that one partner has deserted the other for at least 2 years.

When one or both partners no longer wish to live together, they can either end their marriage by divorce, or separate, keeping the marriage legally alive. A separation may simply mean living apart, or it can be made more formal through a court order.

When one or both partners decide to divorce, an application is made to the local county court or, in London, the Divorce Registry. It is usually made through a solicitor, but can be done by one of the partners alone (but not until at least one year after the date of marriage). If both partners can agree over their finances and together make satisfactory plans for the care of their children, it will probably not be necessary for either to appear in court. Nor will there be any publicity in the papers. There are thousands of divorces each year, and the press cannot report the case unless the divorce is contested or reporting restrictions are lifted.

When the District Judge is satisfied that the appropriate arrangements have been made, that all the information is correct and that the marriage has broken down and cannot be saved, he or she will grant a *decree nisi* - the first stage in obtaining the divorce. Six weeks later, the person seeking the divorce can apply for a *decree absolute.* When this is granted, the marriage comes to an end.

The divorce law has recently been altered, but the changes will not come into force until late 1999 or early in the year 2000 (see right).

CITIZENSHIP FOUNDATION

The new law

When the *Family Law Act 1996* comes into force, there will be only one ground for divorce - that the marriage has irretrievably broken down. There will be no need, as there is now, to give evidence of adultery, unreasonable behaviour, desertion, or that the couple have lived apart for a certain length of time.

Instead, the couple will be required to attend an informal meeting (either separately or together), where they will be given information on counselling, mediation and the process of divorce. If, after a period of at least three months, either or both partners still wish to go ahead with the divorce, they must give a formal statement to the court explaining why their marriage has broken down and cannot be saved.

A compulsory period of reflection follows this - lasting 18 months if the couple have a child under 16, and nine months if they do not.

At the end of this period, if either or both of the people still wish to go ahead with the divorce, the marriage will be ended with a divorce order, provided the court is satisfied with the arrangements that have been made for any children and the couple's finances.

Children

Parents going through a divorce are encouraged to reach an agreement between themselves over where their children will live and how often they will see each parent. But the judge will accept these arrangements only if satisfied that they are in the best interests of the child. If the child is felt to be old enough to have a view of their own, the judge will talk to them in private.

Parents who cannot agree over this are advised not to go straight to court (expensive and stressful for all concerned), but to use independent counsellors to help them sort out their problems. A court will, however, have to approve the final arrangements over children and money. It's usually felt to be in the children's interest to keep in touch with their family, so a judge will rarely stop a parent from seeing a child.

After the divorce, both parents normally keep parental responsibility for their child, and both should consult each other over decisions that affect their child's life, such as education, medical treatment and religious upbringing.

Divorce

Step-parents

Step-parents do not have *parental responsibility* for their stepchildren. With their new partner, the step-parent may help with day to day things affecting the child, but major decisions should be taken by the child's birth mother and father - or only the mother, if they were not married (unless the father has parental responsibility). To change this, a step-parent may apply for parental responsibility or, together with the birthparent, to adopt the child. See **Contacts** for organisation able to give more information about this.

Grandparents

When a marriage ends, it may mean that a child is prevented from seeing other family members, such as grandparents, adding to the child's loss. In this situation, grandparents can apply to a court for permission to carry on seeing the child or to have the child stay with them - although this is more difficult to obtain than for parents.

Family disputes

Sometimes parents become involved in legal disputes which directly affect their children - especially if they are getting divorced and cannot agree who the children should live with. In really important cases a young person who shows enough understanding of the issues, can act on their own initiative to instruct a solicitor and even make an application to the Court. It is usually much better if their views can be reflected through a counsellor or mediator as the whole process can be very stressful and damaging to relationships with parents or other family members. It is important to get specialist advice, see **Contacts**.

Violence

A court can make an order, called an *injunction*, to protect a victim of domestic violence and can order one partner to leave the home for the other's protection - even if they are married. It is important for anyone in this situation to get advice from a solicitor as soon as possible.

CONTACTS See PAGES 119-127 for organisations able to give help & advice

A place of your own

Finding somewhere to live is not always easy. Try to give yourself time to organise the move, and be prepared for a lot of extra expense, particularly at the start.

Where do you look?

Local newspapers, supermarkets and the student union, if you are at college, all carry advertisements. You can also try estate agents and accommodation agencies. The local council housing department can tell you whether you are likely to qualify for council housing, and can also give you details of local housing associations. If it is available to you, university accommodation is usually cheaper and safer.

Estate and accommodation agencies are not allowed, by law, to charge you for information about housing or lists of vacancies. Don't agree to pay them a fee. Normally they are paid for their services by the landlord. If you are asked for money and have any doubts, check first with the local Citizens Advice Bureau or trading standards department. Don't be rushed. It's a good idea to get someone to look at the place with you.

You can't buy or rent a house or get a mortgage until you're 18.

What do you need to know?

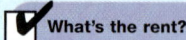

What's the rent? What does it include - council tax, electricity etc.? How often is it paid, and who is it paid to? Is any rent payable in advance? Rent paid in advance will be lost if you leave without giving the right amount of notice.

Your rent is fixed at whatever rate you agreed with your landlord. If you think the rent is too high you can ask your local *rent assessment committee* (ring your local council, or see under 'rent officer' in the phone book) to decide what is reasonable for the property. There is no charge for this, but the committee can only consider this if there are enough similar flats or houses being let in your area.

The rate fixed by the rent assessment committee applies for the remainder of the fixed term of the tenancy but a tenant can make only one application to the committee. It's a good idea to take advice before you do this. Sometimes the committee can put the rate up as well as down.

Do I pay a deposit? This is an amount (often equal to a month's rent) paid to the landlord, or the agent, at the start of the tenancy. Always ask for a receipt when you hand over your deposit.

If you cause damage or leave bills or rent unpaid, the landlord can take what you owe from your deposit. Try to agree any deductions with the landlord before you leave, otherwise you may find you've lost more of your deposit than you should.

Is there a service charge? This is money paid to look after the building and clean those parts which are shared, such as the stairs and corridors in a block of flats. Check what is covered by this figure and decide whether it seems

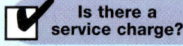

reasonable. If you rent your home from a private landlord or a housing association and pay a variable service charge as well as rent, you have the right to ask the landlord exactly how the service charge is calculated.

☑ Do I need references?

If so, choose people who have known you for a reasonable length of time (a teacher or family friend), but preferably not a close relative. Ask the person concerned first. You may also need references to hire a TV or video for your home.

☑ How safe?

Check the fire escape, plumbing, electrical fittings and heating appliances. Landlords must, by law, have all gas appliances checked each year and must get a certificate of safety which you are entitled to see.

Housing Benefit

If you are on Youth Training, Income Support or a low wage, you may qualify for Housing Benefit from your local council. Your local housing advice centre or Citizens Advice Bureau can help you work out what you're entitled to. Housing Benefit is not available to full-time students, unless they have children or have a disability.

If you're out of work and on Housing Benefit, you may find that you lose your Housing Benefit when you start working - which could make it difficult to keep on your flat or house.

Housing Benefit for most single people will not be more than the average rent of a single room in the area.

Leaving home

Young people under 18 are still, in law, in the "custody and care" of their parents, which means that, strictly speaking, they need their parent's permission to leave home. But, in reality, courts are unlikely to order anyone aged 16 or 17 to return home who leaves home against their parents' wishes, unless they appear to be in some kind of danger or unable to look after themeselves. See also **Family**, page 62.

If you are 16 or 17 and homeless, or feel that you can no longer live at home because you are being hurt, or because life at home is so bad, you can get help from social services. Under the *Children Act 1989*, local authorities must provide accommodation for 16 and 17 year olds who are in need or whose welfare would be endangered if accommodation was not provided. However, some local authorities find it difficult to get hold of suitable accommodation for young people, and Income Support is not available to all 16 or 17 year olds. Therefore, if you can, get advice from a housing advice centre, Citizens Advice Bureau or your local council before you do anything.

In care

If you are leaving care, your local social services have a legal duty to provide help and advice.

Tenancy agreements

When you rent a flat or house, you normally sign an agreement with the landlord or their agent. This is known in law as a *tenancy agreement*, sometimes called a *lease*.

It should contain all the conditions agreed between you and the landlord, along with a list (called an *inventory*) of the furniture and other equipment that comes with the property. Make sure everything is included, and make a note of anything that's damaged when you take up the property. Read all documents carefully. Don't be afraid to seek advice from the Citizens Advice Bureau, a housing advice centre or a solicitor if parts are not clear, or if they contain conditions which you didn't expect. Don't sign until you fully understand the agreement and are prepared to accept what it says.

Normally you and the landlord will each sign, exchange and keep a copy of the tenancy agreement. Look after this. If there's any kind of problem while you're in the property, you'll need it to check your rights and duties.

Assured shorthold tenancy

This is the name given to the kind of tenancy that you will probably have if you rent a house or a flat. In fact, if your tenancy agreement was made on or after 28 February 1997, it must be of this type, unless you have some kind of written statement from the landlord saying it is not.

Your tenancy agreement will probably work like this....

● You are "assured" of the right to stay as a tenant for the period stated in the agreement, unless you break the agreement in some way, in which case the landlord can apply to a court to get you to leave earlier. Assured shorthold tenancies used to be for a period of at least six months. This minimum period no longer applies.

● You can't leave before the end of this time, without being required to pay the balance of the rent, unless your tenancy agreement has a "break clause" allowing you to leave early by serving an agreed period of notice, such as one month. You can ask for this to be included in your agreement.

● You have a right to receive from your landlord a written statement of the terms of your tenancy. This includes the date that the tenancy began, the date that it ends, the amount of rent payable and the date that it is due. The landlord can be prosecuted and fined if this information is not provided within 28

Lodging and hostels

You do not have the same rights if you are in lodgings or if your landlord lives with you in the same house and shares the basic services with you. Your landlady or landlord only needs to give you "reasonable notice" (this can be seven days), and does not need to apply to a court to have you evicted.

If you are in hostel accommodation with a local council or housing association, they will not generally need a court order to evict you. They can give you notice at any time, as long as they keep to the terms of the tenancy agreement.

Council tenants

You have certain rights as a council tenant, which include staying in your house for as long as you want (assuming you pay your rent and do what your tenancy agreement says), taking in lodgers, and being

consulted about the running of the estate. The council has a right to take action against tenants who cause a nuisance to others on the estate. In serious cases this has led to tenants losing their homes, see page 20. Further information is given in the *Council Tenant's Charter*, see **Contacts**.

days of your request.

- The landlord must give you at least two months' notice to leave. With a six month tenancy this will normally be at the end of the fourth month.
- If the landlord delays this and does not serve notice until the fifth or sixth month, or even later, you have the right (assuming you continue to pay the rent), to stay in the property for a further two months.
- If you stay on without the landlord's permission after the two months' notice has expired, the landlord is entitled to apply to a court for an order to have you evicted. This will almost certainly be granted, and you will then be expected to pay the costs of the court order as well as

the rent for the extra time in the property. It is illegal for a landlord to evict you without a court order (see Eviction below).

- If you take on an assured shorthold tenancy remember that you are legally responsible for the rent up to the end of the agreed period. If you are sharing the flat or house with someone and they leave, then their share of the rent must still be paid until a replacement is found.
- If you're a student, make sure that your tenancy agreement lasts at least as long as your academic year - otherwise you may have to look for somewhere to live in the middle of the term.

Tenancy agreements

Repairs and maintenance

Who is responsible?

If your tenancy agreement is for less than seven years, as it almost certainly will be, your landlord is responsible by law for looking after the structure of the building, including outside fittings (such as gutters) and essential services (heating appliances - not cookers - sinks, baths and toilets and the water, gas and electricity supplies). Responsibility for other repairs depends on what is said in the tenancy agreement. Tenants are normally responsible for repairs for damage that they cause, but not for fair "wear and tear".

Getting them done

Tell the landlord when the repairs need doing - and keep paying the rent. If the landlord does nothing and the problem concerns serious questions of health and safety, you can get in touch with the local environmental health office. They have the powers to get something done, and can make the landlord carry out the necessary work. Their number is in the phone book under the name of your local council.

If the problem is not serious, or the local council won't take action, check again that responsibility for the work lies with your landlord. If it does, write to the landlord explaining you intend to undertake the work yourself and send at least two estimates of the cost. Give your landlord at least two weeks to consider these. If, at the end of this period, there is still no sign that the repairs will be carried out, you may go ahead with them yourself, taking the cost from your rent. Keep detailed records of everything you've done and a copy of every letter you write and receive.

Dear Landlord
As I told you by (phone/letter) on (date), the water heater at (the address) is broken, and it is your responsibility to put this right under our tenancy agreement. Since this has not been done, I have got (two) estimates for repairs from (names and addresses of firms), which I enclose. Unless I hear from you by (date) that you will do these repairs straightaway, I will have no option but to ask (name your choice) to do the repair. I shall then deduct their b from future rental payments.
Your sincerely,

Eviction

Generally speaking, you cannot be made to leave the house or flat that you are renting, unless the landlord has given you notice in the correct way and obtained a possession order from a court. In most cases, it is a criminal offence for anyone to evict you without a court order, or to try to force you out with threats. Court orders are not necessary, however, if you live in lodgings or your landlord lives on the premises. But your landlord still can't use violence to force you to leave. This is an offence under the *Criminal Law Act 1977*.

If you're threatened with eviction, get advice straightaway from a solicitor or your local council housing department or Citizens Advice Bureau. Make sure you keep on paying the rent. Failure to pay will make it easier for the landlord to require you to leave.

Harassment

If your landlord stops short of physical violence, but still behaves in a way designed to make you leave - like changing the locks, shouting abuse or playing loud music - they will be breaking the *Protection from Eviction Act 1977*. Again your local council, housing advice centre or Citizens Advice Bureau can help. If physical violence is used or threatened, call the police.

A few weeks after signing a six month tenancy agreement for a bed-sit, Laurie was told to leave. His landlord had decided to sell the house and knew he would get more money for it with Laurie out of his room. The lock on Laurie's door was taken off, and the landlord threatened to tip his possessions into a black plastic bag. Without a job, Laurie spent more than two months sleeping in his car. With legal advice, and using legal aid, he took his case to court. The judge decided Laurie had been illegally evicted and ordered the landlord to pay him £36,500 in compensation - the extra amount of money the landlord made by selling his house without a tenant.

Discrimination

A landlord must not discriminate against a would-be tenant on grounds of race or sex, unless the property is being shared with others, and the landlord (or close relatives) live at the property. It is also against the law for someone who sells or lets property to discriminate against a disabled person. Landlords and members of their immediate family who let out rooms to less than seven people in their own homes are not affected.

Insurance

If you are living in rented accommodation, insurance for the *building* is normally arranged by the owner, but it's worth checking exactly what this covers. Building insurance will not cover the cost of replacing your things if they are damaged or stolen. You can arrange to insure your belongings through an insurance company or a broker, see **Money**, page 56.

If you have anything valuable, like a camera, stereo or jewellery, you will need to list it separately on the insurance and find out exactly how much it costs to replace. The same applies to something like a bike which may be stolen or lost outside the home.

Some policies will give you the full replacement cost, others take into account wear and tear, and pay you less. If you are under insured it means that your belongings are insured for less than their real value. If this is discovered by the insurance company when you make a claim, the amount they pay out is likely to be reduced.

Noisy neighbours

The best way to tackle a problem of noise, or any other nuisance, is to talk to the person concerned, if possible, before the situation gets out of hand. Sometimes this is easier and more effective if several people complain together. If this doesn't work, write a simple letter (keep a copy), and allow a reasonable time for your neighbour to respond.

If that fails, get in touch with your local environmental health department which has powers to investigate and deal with the matter, under the *Environmental Protection Act 1990*. See also Leisure, page 84.

Homeless

If you are homeless, the council housing department should be able to help. It has a legal duty to give you advice and help towards finding somewhere to live, but this is not the same as offering you somewhere to stay. The council has to house you only if you are 16 or over and

- **homeless;** *and*
- **in priority need;** *and*
- **have a connection with the local area;** *and*
- **have not made yourself intentionally homeless.**

You should qualify as a priority need if

- **you're pregnant, or think you might be; or**
- **you have a child; or**
- **you've had to leave your last home because someone was violent towards you; or**
- **you've lost your home through something like a fire or flood; or**
- **your age, health problems or disability make you vulnerable and unable to cope with being homeless.**

Just being young and alone does not mean you qualify automatically. Some local authorities will recognise all 16 or 17 year olds as being vulnerable, but others will only consider certain groups, such as those who have left local authority care. Seek advice from Shelter or other housing advice centres. You might also get help from Social Services.

Sleeping rough

This is dangerous, and places you at risk of being assaulted. Without an address, it is harder to get a job and even benefit. If you're in this position, try to get advice (see above).

It may also be an offence. Under the *Vagrancy Act 1824*, someone found sleeping rough or begging more than once may be fined.

Squatting

A squatter is someone who enters and occupies land, or any part of a building, without the owner's permission. Squatting is not a crime, but squatters may commit an offence if they cause damage when getting into the property, or by using gas or electricity without first making the proper arrangements.

Squatting is often insecure. If the place is left empty, the owner can break in and take possession, but commits an offence if force is used while the squatters are still inside. An owner or tenant who intends to move in immediately and use the property as a place of residence, may use reasonable force in getting a squatter to leave, but normally requires a written statement or certificate showing that the property is needed as a home. In this situation a squatter commits an offence in refusing to leave.

Squatters can also be evicted from a property through the issue of a possession order by a court. There are a number of different types of order but, in some circumstances, squatters may have only 24 hours to leave and may not return to the property within the next twelve months.

Advice is available for anyone considering squatting. See Contacts for details.

LEISURE

78 GOING OUT

82 GETTING BACK

83 STAYING IN

85 SPORT

86 THE OPEN AIR

88 ANIMALS

young citizen's **passport**

Going out

It may be for fun, but you don't leave your legal rights at home when you go out for the night. If you spend an evening at a match or concert looking at nothing more than a roof support or girder, then you have a right to complain and ask for a refund. It's no excuse for the management to say that you should have arrived earlier for a better seat. Under the law of contract they should have warned you that the view was restricted before selling you the tickets.

There is no simple law setting out people's rights in the event of a change to the advertised programme or the cancellation of a performance. Your legal position will depend on such things as advance publicity, information given when the ticket was sold and the circumstances that forced a change of plan.

Although disgruntled spectators have been successful in taking promoters to court, legal action is not recommended for disappointment over a cancelled event. Some promoters will try to retain some goodwill by offering tickets for another performance, or refunds. If they don't, it's worth explaining why you think their action is *unreasonable* - a key word in cases of this kind.

Pubs and off-licences

The licensing laws controlling the sale of drinks were introduced in the First World War, and it's only in the last few years that they have begun to change.

Providing they sell soft drinks and food, pubs can now apply for a children's certificate allowing children under 14, accompanied by an adult, into a bar. The children, however, have to leave by 9pm.

Once you're 14, it's legal for you to go into the bar of a pub, but only for soft drinks and at the licensee's discretion. At 16, or over, you can buy beer, cider or perry (made from pear juice), but only to drink with a meal in the dining or restaurant area of a pub.

Only when you're 18 can you buy alcohol or drink alcohol in a bar. Drinks with 0.5% or less of alcohol, such as some canned shandy and low alcohol beers, are treated as non-alcoholic.

It is an offence to sell alcohol to anyone under 18 - unless it can be shown that the landlord did their best to check the person was 18 or over. It's also an offence for you to buy, or try to buy, alcohol if you are under 18, or to buy or try to buy it for someone under 18. The maximum fine for this is £1000, and licensees stand to lose their licence after more than one conviction.

The measures of alcohol that you can be sold are legally controlled. However, until section 43 of the *Weights and Measures Act 1985* finally comes into force, the froth on the top of a glass of beer still forms part of the pint. The prices of drinks and food should be displayed by law, and should be clearly visible from where the drinks are served.

Refusing to serve

Pubs and off-licences can refuse to serve anyone with drink who looks as if they've had enough already, otherwise they can be charged with 'permitting drunkenness' and fined.

Licensees have the right to ban or refuse to serve anyone they choose, regardless of their age - unless it is for reasons of sex, colour, ethnic group or disability.

Not on the streets

A number of towns and cities now ban the drinking of alcohol in public. Under local by-laws, anyone who refuses to stop drinking in the street, when asked by a police officer, risks arrest and a fine of up to £500.

Proof of age

If you have trouble proving you are over 18, you can apply for a *proof of age card*, carrying your name, photograph, date of birth and signature. It's run by the Portman Group - an organisation sponsored by Britain's major drinks companies - and it's free. Application forms are available from pubs, off-licences and supermarkets. See **Contacts** for details.

Confiscating alcohol

If the police find a young person under 18, in a public place or a place they have entered illegally, and believe that they have been drinking, or are about to drink, they can, under the *Confiscation of Alcohol (Young Persons) Act 1997*, take away and destroy the alcohol.

They can also take alcohol from someone *over* 18 who is in a public place, if they believe it will be passed to under-age drinkers.

The police can ask for the name and address of anyone from whom they have taken alcohol in these circumstances, and it is an offence to refuse to give these details or to give the police a false name and address.

Eating out

Quality

Whether you're in an expensive restaurant or an ordinary takeaway you have the right to reject any food of a quality below the standard that you are reasonably entitled to expect. What is 'reasonable' depends on such things as the price charged, what the menu says, and basic standards. The laws applying to faulty goods or services also apply here. (See **Money**, page 48).

Complaints

It's advisable to complain as soon as you know there's a problem. The more you are paying the higher the standard you're entitled to expect.

If the quality of your meal is poor or the service is bad, you are entitled to make a reasonable deduction from the bill, but don't leave without paying. Explain to the manager why you are not satisfied, and leave your name and address. It is then up to the restaurant to take this up with you later on if they wish.

Price

All restaurants, pubs and cafés must, by law, clearly display the price of food and drink where it is served, so you can read it before you order or sit down at a table.

Service charge

A service charge, usually 10%, is sometimes added to the bill in a restaurant. If this was made clear *before* you ordered, then you've got to pay it, unless the service was really bad. In that case, see the manager and ask for a discount. If there is no service charge, it's up to you whether to leave a tip.

Booking

If you decide to book a table and don't show up, the restaurant is entitled to make a charge if it has not been able to fill the table. If, on the other hand, you book a table which has not been kept when you arrive, you can ask for compensation for the cost of the wasted journey.

Safety

Under the *Food Act 1990*, it is a criminal offence for a restaurant to serve food that is unfit for human consumption. If you are concerned about the hygiene in a place where you have eaten, you can contact your local environmental health office, which has the power to investigate such cases.

Going out

Raves

People who organise raves need an entertainment licence, and to get this the event must meet certain safety standards. Many raves are legal and are arranged in conjunction with the local licensing authorities. Illegal raves however are unlicensed and often without adequate safety precautions. These are more likely to be dangerous, particularly if there is overcrowding.

Under the *Criminal Justice and Public Order Act 1994*, the police have the power to break up an unlicensed open air rave of more than 100 people if it seems that the noise and disturbance are likely to cause distress to the local inhabitants. This means that, under the orders of a senior police officer, the police can order off the land anyone who is preparing, waiting for, or attending the rave. They can also seize and confiscate any sound equipment that is being used. Anyone who goes back onto the land within seven days can be fined or imprisoned for up to three months.

The police can also stop anyone within five miles of the rave, and order them not to proceed to the gathering. Anyone who refuses to turn back may be fined. Although the police have the powers to close raves and unlicensed parties that break the law, many forces prefer to get involved only if there is a danger to people's safety or a serious nuisance.

Taking Ecstasy causes a rise in body temperature. If, in addition, it's hot inside the building and people are dancing there is a danger of dehydration or heatstroke if body fluid is not replaced. It's advisable therefore to drink about a pint of water every hour and to take regular breaks. Alcohol doesn't help, as it dehydrates the body even further. For more information on drugs and the law, see **Life**, page 10.

Nightclubs

Nightclubs must have special licences for entertainment and the sale of alcohol. Like pubs, it's illegal to sell alcohol to someone under 18 and owners are within their rights to choose who they will or will not allow in, as long as they do not break the sex, race or disability

discrimination laws. Clubs who charge lower entry fees for women than men are breaking the law.

The door

Bouncers have no special powers. The same laws apply to them as everyone else, which means that they can only use a reasonable amount of force to throw someone out. In certain circumstances this means no force at all - and a bouncer who uses too much force without good reason commits an offence.

Gambling

There are no age restrictions on who can play fruit and slot machines in amusement arcades and fairs, but many arcades have a voluntary code that excludes under 18s. The minimum legal pay out is 70p, in the pound - although machines are usually set a little higher than this. Maximum prizes are restricted to £10 in cash.

Lottery tickets or scratch cards should not be sold to anyone under the age of 16, nor can the winnings be collected by someone below this age.

If you're under 18, you are not allowed into a casino, betting shop - or a licensed bingo club, unless you are only going in to watch. Gambling contracts cannot be enforced in law. If the loser fails to pay, he or she cannot be taken to court. Therefore, if you bet, it's wise to use a reputable bookie.

Fireworks

The age at which a person can buy fireworks has been raised to 18. It is also an offence to sell fireworks to anyone who appears to be under 18.

Rave On!

hard!

Getting back

Black cabs, licensed taxis

These are subject to tight licensing control. The vehicles must be checked regularly, the fares are set by law and the drivers may have had to sit an exam to get their licence. Black cabs can be flagged down as well as hired from a taxi rank.

Under the *Disability Discrimination Act 1995*, newly licensed taxis in most areas have to be fully accessible to disabled travellers. Black cab and licensed taxi drivers are also required to help disabled people in and out of taxis and to help with their luggage - although drivers can claim exemption from these regulations if they have a back injury that prevents them from lifting heavy objects.

 No Entry The driver of a licensed taxi or private hire car who refuses to take a disabled passenger may be prosecuted and fined under the *Town Police Clauses Act 1847*. Anyone who feels that they are a victim of this, and wishes to do something about it, should make a note of the plate or registration number of the taxi or private hire vehicle and report it to their local licensing authority. (The main local council switchboard can provide the number.) The licensing authority will investigate the case and then prosecute the driver if they feel there is sufficient evidence.

Minicabs, private hire cars

If you want a private hire car, you should either book it in advance or wait your turn in the cab office. If you do succeed in flagging one down, you may not be covered by insurance if there's a crash. Even if there's a meter, get an estimate of the fare before you set off. If there isn't, always agree the fare in advance. Minicabs and private hire cars are generally unaffected by the *Disability Discrimination Act*.

Unlicensed taxis

Unlike black cabs or licensed taxis, these vehicles will not have been specially examined and may not even have a current MOT. Neither will they be insured to carry passengers for private hire purposes.

Staying in

cannabis on the premises, can be convicted of allowing the place to be used for the smoking of cannabis. For more on the law and drugs, see **Life** pages 10.

Safety You invite some friends around for the evening and one of them falls down the stairs. If the cause of the accident was the state of the carpet rather than too much beer, you or your parents could be liable for his injuries. This doesn't mean wrapping every sharp corner in cotton wool, but something like a loose piece of stair carpet definitely should be fixed, since it is reasonable for visitors to expect to walk down the stairs safely. You're not expected to guard against the *unforeseeable*. If someone slides down the bannisters and breaks a leg, then that's their problem.

Insurance If someone is injured in your home you could be required to pay them compensation - although this can be paid through an insurance policy, if you have one. Most householders' insurance policies cover owners for injuries to other people called "third parties" caused by the state of the buildings or its fittings. If you're in rented accommodation, your landlord could be liable - and again it is their insurance company that would pay damages. If you face this problem, it's worth checking with a solicitor.

Parties

Drink and drugs Although you can't buy alcohol from an off-licence until you're 18, anyone over five can drink alcohol on private premises. It is an offence to give alcohol to a child under five, unless given by a doctor on health grounds.

An offence is committed, under the *Misuse of Drugs Act 1971*, if you knowingly allow anyone into your flat or house to supply an illegal drug to someone else, or allow the smoking of cannabis. Even if you are not taking the drug yourself, you can still be charged, as it is your place they are using. However, two sisters, aged 17 and 20 who lived with their parents and had a party while they were away, were found not guilty of allowing people to smoke cannabis after their guests were arrested for using the drug. The Court decided that the sisters did not have legal possession of their parents' house and were not occupiers as they would have been if it had been their own flat or house. But, Courts have decided that a person who shares a flat or house with someone who they know smokes

Staying in

TV, video, music and games

Gatecrashing

Gatecrashing is *trespass*. The law says that you can use reasonable force to get gatecrashers to leave, but don't start waving a broken bottle around. This is unreasonable and will leave you in more trouble for them. Nor are you responsible for the safety of gatecrashers - your *duty of care* only covers those you have invited or allowed in to your home.

Noise

If there is a noisy party and the police are called, they can ask people to be quiet, but there's not much else they can do unless they fear there's going to be a *breach of the peace* - that is some kind of disorder. Then arrests will almost certainly be made.

However, if you are being disturbed by noise from a neighbour between 11pm and 7am, you can ring the local environmental health department which must investigate your complaint as soon as possible. Under the *Noise Act 1996*, they have the power to send an officer to the house to measure the noise and decide whether it is excessive. If it is, the person responsible will be given a warning notice, requiring the noise to be switched off or turned down within ten minutes. An offence is committed if the noise continues, and the officer can decide to prosecute or issue an on the spot fine of £100.

If the warning notice is ignored, the environmental health officer can obtain a warrant (often very quickly), to go into the building and remove the sound equipment that is being used.

For other problems with noisy neighbours, see the section on **Home**, page 75.

A *licence* is required if anyone in a household uses a television or video recorder. One licence covers everything in the home, and this also applies to a group of people sharing a house together. But someone who rents a separate room in a house is not covered by their landlord's licence. They will need a licence of their own. A person with a TV in a second home should have a second TV licence.

Copyright

Copyright laws give writers, artists, publishers etc. the right to take action against anyone who makes a copy of, or broadcasts their work without permission. Breaking copyright is treated in law like a form of theft, but the law is only usually enforced against people who are making illegal copies and selling them.

Books, plays and music are protected by copyright law for 70 years after the author's death. Computer generated work and broadcasts are covered for 50 years from the time that they were made.

You can make a tape of a TV or radio broadcast for your own use, but only to allow you to listen to it at a more convenient time. Strictly speaking, it's against the law to record a programme that you intend to keep as part of a collection or because you find it particularly interesting or enjoyable. Copying a CD, tape or computer game belonging to someone else is also illegal.

Sport

A Stockport County player was awarded £250,000 after his career was ended through injuries suffered in a match against Swansea City. The court decided that he was brought down by a tackle aimed at the legs, rather than the ball, which did not reflect the reasonable care that players should show towards one another.

Safety

The Bradford fire, the tragedy at Hillsborough and other disturbances, particularly at football matches, led to a number of laws controlling sports events.

It's an offence to be drunk at a football match or to have alcoholic drinks in the ground, and even on a supporters' coach or train travelling to or from the event. At the moment the law only applies to football.

Risks and the duty of care

Anyone who plays sport must expect to suffer the sorts of injuries normal to the game concerned. But *intentional* or *reckless damage* to someone else is another matter, and the player responsible can be sued for damages and prosecuted for a criminal offence. Organisers of sporting events also have a duty to see that visitors, spectators and passers-by are reasonably safe.

A rugby player was convicted of causing grievous bodily harm after kicking an opponent on the head following a tackle by another player. He was sentenced to 18 months in prison. He appealed against the length of the sentence, but the Court of Appeal said that, in the circumstances, the sentence was fair and reasonable.

The open air

Walking

All land in the United Kingdom is owned by someone - private landowners, a local authority, government body (eg ministry of defence), or the Crown, (the Queen).

Stepping on to a piece of land marked "*trespassers will be prosecuted*" will not propel you straight into court. Trespass is not a crime (unless you also cause damage) - it's a civil offence. A landowner can require the trespasser to leave, but in doing so may use only a reasonable amount of force. If the trespasser refuses to go, the landowner should call the police.

Footpaths

If a route across a piece of land has been used for 20 years or more without interruption, that route becomes a right of way. A footpath cannot be lost through disuse. Once a right of way has been established it can be used by the public forever or until it is closed by an order made under the *Highways Act 1980* or the *Town and Country Planning Act 1990*.

Strictly speaking, footpaths are for walkers only. It's a criminal offence to drive a motor bike or car on a path. Footpaths are shown on Ordnance Survey maps - but if you need to check on a path, you can ask to look at the maps in the local council planning office. Under the *Rights of Way Act 1990*, when land is ploughed or any crop (except grass) is planted over a public footpath, the landowner must, within 14 days, make sure that the line of the path is clear to anyone using it. It is also an offence to put up a misleading sign, such as "private" that discourages people from using a public right of way. If you come across a problem of this kind and want something done, contact the landowner, or the local council.

The local council's Rights of Way Officer has a duty to make sure that public rights of way are kept open and free from obstruction. It's the local council's responsibility to maintain footpaths so that people can walk along them, and the job of the landowner to look after stiles and gates along the path.

The Government has said that it plans to give the public more access to upland areas by giving walkers a "right to roam" - although, at first, they shall probably try to do this not through law but with the voluntary agreement of landowners. More information is available from the Countryside Commission, see **Contacts** for details.

Bulls

Checking your legal rights here needs some farming knowledge and the ability to tell one breed of bull from another without getting too close. All dairy bulls (that's breeds like Friesian, Guernsey and Jersey) are banned from fields crossed by public paths. Other types of bull are allowed only if they are in with cows or heifers, which apparently makes them much less aggressive.

Rivers, canals and the sea

There is a public right to use a canoe or boat only on the *tidal* section of a river. Beyond this point you need permission from the owner of the river bank to use the river.

You also need a licence to use a boat or canoe on a canal - obtainable from British Waterways (the number of your local office will be in the phone book) and the British Canoe Union.

Anyone is free to use a boat or to water-ski or jet-ski on the sea although, in harbours, ferries and other shipping have a right of way.

Fishing

You can fish in the sea and in tidal waters at any time, unless there are local by-laws forbidding it. Fishing off a pier usually needs a licence.

Anyone aged twelve or over who fishes for salmon, trout, freshwater fish or eels must have an Environment Agency Rod Fishing Licence, available from post offices. The licence allows the holder to fish anywhere in England and Wales, but permission is still required from the landowner or the person owning the fishing rights.

Pollution

The Environment Agency asks members of the public to report any environmental incident - on rivers, lakes, canals or the coastline - or the dumping of rubbish, by ringing their local Environment Agency office (in the phone book) or by using the free

Katrina noticed that the water in Ackhurst Brook near Wigan, where she lived, was an unusual colour - particularly around the discharge pipe used by a local factory. She rang the Environment Agency who sent an officer to investigate. The officer reported that the water was discoloured and smelt foul and contained pieces of food that looked like shells from baked beans - which is just what they were. The company admitted polluting the river and was fined £5,000 by local magistrates.

24 hour number, 0800 80 70 60.

Beaches

Land between the low and high tide lines is the property of the Crown - but there is almost never a problem in walking along a beach. However, there is no right to get onto a beach over private land, unless there is a public right of way.

Animals

Wildlife

The *Wildlife and Countryside Act 1981* gives protection to a wide range of wild animals, birds and plants and covers killing, injuring, taking or possessing and disturbing the place of shelter or protection. For an up-to-date list of all protected species, see Whitakers Almanack, available in most libraries. The *Wild Mammals (Protection) Act 1996* makes it an offence to inflict unnecessary suffering on any wild mammal.

Pets

It is an offence to sell a pet animal to anyone below the age of 12. Under the *Protection of Animals Act 1911*, a pet owner has a legal responsibility to care for the animal and make sure it does not suffer unnecessarily. It is an offence to be cruel to the animal or to abandon it if it is likely to cause the animal unnecessary suffering.

Pet owners are also responsible for any damage their animal causes if they knew (or should have known) it was likely to cause such damage, or if their animal is defined as *dangerous*.

Dangerous animals are known, in law, as those that are not domesticated in this country and might be expected to have dangerous characteristics, such as a monkey or snake. Anyone keeping an animal of this kind must have a licence.

When Lisa had to go away unexpectedly, she said that she asked a friend to feed and water her pet rat, Ziggy. After Lisa had been gone for six days, one of Lisa's neighbour told the RSPCA that the animal was in need of care. They found the rat with just a scrap of cheese and no water. It was dehydrated, trembling and close to death. Lisa, who was unemployed, was fined £80 and told to pay £50 towards the cost of the case.

Dogs

Under the Control of Dogs Order 1992, anyone owning a dog must make sure that it wears a collar with the name and address of its owner when it is in a public place. If a dog fouls a footpath, the person in charge of the dog commits an offence if he or she fails to clear up the mess.

It is an offence under the Dangerous Dogs Act 1991, to allow a dog to be dangerously out of control in a public place. The owner, or person in charge, of the dog can be fined or imprisoned for up to six months. The court can also order the dog to be destroyed, and can disqualify the owner from keeping a dog in the future. A farmer is allowed to shoot a dog that is not under anyone's control and is worrying livestock on their land.

Under the Guard Dog Act 1975, guard dogs should be under the control of a handler or else tied up and not able to roam freely. A warning notice should also be displayed. The Act does not apply to dogs guarding private houses or farm land.

CONTACTS See PAGES 119-127 for organisations able to give help & advice

TRAVEL
& TRANSPORT

90 HOLIDAYS
92 BUSES & TRAINS

94 CARS & MOTORBIKES
98 DRIVING

100 ACCIDENTS

young citizen's passport

Holidays

Package holidays

When you book a holiday, you are making a contract with the tour organiser - that is the company responsible for arranging the package. This is usually the tour operator, but it can also be the travel agent, particularly if you have asked for extra arrangements to be made, not included in the brochure.

Although holiday brochures are designed to show the hotel or resort at its best, the *Package Travel, Package Holidays and Package Tours Regulations 1992* state that they must be accurate and not misleading. If the room or the swimming pool that you were promised are not available, you may be able to claim compensation because of the failure of the company arranging the holiday to keep its side of the contract. It is an offence, under the *Trade Descriptions Act 1968*, for a firm to make a statement about the goods or services it provides that it knows to be false - but prosecution for this is usually taken up by local trading standards officers.

It's important to tell the travel agent or tour operator if you have any special needs at the time you make the booking.

Before you sign or hand over any money, it's important to read the small print and to check what it says about changes to your schedule. Under certain circumstances, travel organisers can alter flight times or accommodation arrangements *provided they make this clear in the brochure or contract*. If you pay all or part of the cost of the holiday by credit card, you may be entitled to claim a full or partial refund from the credit card company if the firm organising the holiay fails to keep its

side of the contract. For more information on paying by credit card, see page 52.

If you go abroad, book through a travel company registered with ABTA, IATA or ATOL. If the travel firm belongs to one of these organisations, you'll find their symbol in the brochure. They will cover the cost of getting you home, or compensate you for your losses if the company you've booked with goes bust while you're away, or before you've left.

Before you go

- Check whether you need to have any vaccinations, and think about getting medical insurance, see below.
- If you are travelling in the European Community, get Form E111 at a main post office - allowing you free or reduced medical costs - and take the form with you on holiday.
- Check your passport is up to date and whether you need a visa for the country you are visiting. Passports are not needed for travel to the Republic of Ireland.
- If you're thinking of hitching, check on advisability before you go. In some countries it is illegal.

If you need to know more about travel requirements or conditions, ring the embassy of the country concerned, or contact the Foreign and Commonwealth Office, tel 0171 238 4503.

Travel and medical insurance

A good travel insurance policy will protect you from losses while you're away and even illness before you go, but check that it covers the sorts of things you are planning to do. If not, take out extra cover. If you are ill or hurt, you may have to pay for treatment yourself and then claim the money back

Having a lovely time...

...wish you were

when you get home. Make sure you keep receipts and other documents as evidence for your claim.

Take the policy with you on holiday, so that if anything goes wrong you can make sure you keep to the terms of the agreement.

Passports   A passport costs £21 and is valid for 10 years in any country of the world. However, some countries require visitors' passports to be valid for a period of time *beyond* their stay - and this can be for as much as a year. Therefore if your passport is in, or nearing, its final year, you may need to apply for another.

You must have your own passport, unless you are under 16 and travelling with your parents on theirs'. If you are under 16, and need your own passport, your parent's consent is needed on the application form.

If something goes wrong

If there is a problem with the holiday that the travel company has provided, tell them or their representative as soon as possible. If you're still not satisfied, make a note of the facts (photographic evidence may be helpful), and then contact the travel firm as soon as you get home.

If you're not satisfied with their reply, write politely, but firmly, to the managing director of the travel firm. If the company belongs to ABTA, you can have your claim decided by an independent person called an arbitrator. If this is not possible, get advice from the Citizens Advice Bureau and, if necessary, a local solicitor. Going to court is a last resort.

If your luggage doesn't arrive, report the loss immediately. Try to obtain a copy of any reports that you complete. Under international law, the airline is responsible for lost or damaged luggage, but compensation is paid by weight rather than value. It may be better to claim through your holiday insurance.

If you run out of money, even overseas, you can go to a bank and arrange for money to be transferred from your own bank or building society at home. There will probably be a charge, but it should arrive within 24 hours.

If you lose anything valuable, tell the police and get a note from them confirming that you have done this. Contact the travel company if you lose your ticket home, and immediately report the loss of traveller's cheques or credit cards to the company offices. They often let you reverse the charges for the call. It is very important to report losses to your insurance company within the time limit stated in the policy.

If your passport is lost or stolen, contact the British Consulate who have an office in most big cities and should be able to provide you with help or advice.

In trouble

Travellers overseas are automatically subject to the laws of the country they are visiting.

If you're arrested insist on the British Consulate being informed. The Consulate will explain the local procedures, including access to a lawyer and the availability of legal aid.

Holidays

Taking a car or motocycle

You'll normally need to get a *Green Card* from your insurance company, which extends your motor insurance to countries other than Great Britain.

If you're driving to Spain, you should also take out a Bail Bond (*fianza*). Under Spanish law, the car and driver can be detained after an accident, but can be released on production of a Bail Bond. The Bond will also help cover the cost of any legal action or fine. Contact your motor insurance company for both the Green Card and Bail Bond.

If you have an accident, tell the police and ask for a record or receipt. It will help with your insurance claim when you get home. For the same reason, it's also a good idea to take notes and photographs of the incident, including pictures of the number plates of the vehicles involved.

Don't sign anything in a language that you don't understand. If you're put under pressure, write "*I don't understand*" immediately above your signature.

Coming home

The amount of goods, particularly alcohol, that you can bring back into Britain depends on the country from which you are returning. The allowances are more generous when returning to Britain from a country inside the European Union, but this may change if the "duty free" system is abolished within the EU.

Customs officials can check your baggage for prohibited goods (such as drugs, weapons or obscene materials), or to see if you need to pay tax or duty (if you are coming from or have travelled through a country outside the European Union). For more details of the rights and duties of customs officers contact your local Customs and Excise office (under "C" in the phone book), or see the Traveller's Charter, available from libraries.

Getting about

Buses and trains

Tickets

By the time you're 16, you have to pay full fare on all buses and trains, trams and the Underground. In some areas full fare is charged on buses from the age of 14.

If you travel on a train or the London Underground without a ticket, you may be charged an on the spot penalty, as well as the cost of your fare. Information about this is displayed in stations where this system is in operation.

If you are stranded at a station without any money for a ticket, your ticket can be bought for you by someone else at another station, with the authorisation sent by telephone to where you are waiting. This is known as a *silk arrangement* .

Some tickets are cheaper when travelling outside the rush hour, and travel cards give you further reductions.

● A Young Persons Railcard costs £18 and entitles you to a third off most ticket prices. Everyone aged 16-25 is eligible to have one, as are students aged 26 and over who attend a UK educational establishment for over 15 hours a week, and at least 20 weeks a year. You can buy the Railcard at large stations, some travel agents and from student services at college.

● An Inter-Rail Pass gives you at least 15 days rail travel in Europe from £159, with discounts available on Eurostar and many cross Channel ferries. You must be under 26, have been resident in Europe for at least six months and have a passport, which you will need when you book. Inter-Rail cards are available from selected stations and travel agents or by contacting Rail Europe, tel 0990 848 848.

● Student Coachcards entitles full time students aged 17-25, and mature students over 25, who study at least 15 hours a week for 20 weeks a year, to a 30% discount on coach journeys. One year cards cost £7, and £18 buys a card valid for three years.

● The Under 26 Youth Card provides members with discounted air fares worldwide, and also offers reductions at home on places to stay and visit. Contact Under 26 on 0171 823 5363.

Getting about

Emma bought a ticket for a day trip to London, saying that she wanted to travel on the next train, leaving in 15 minutes.

When the inspector checked her ticket on the train, she asked Emma to pay a further £6, as she had been undercharged by the booking clerk. Although Emma claimed that it was the train operating company's mistake in selling her the wrong ticket, by law she had to pay the difference. When a contract is made, one side cannot gain by the other side's genuine mistake.

Complaints

If your train (or bus) is late, there's not a lot in law that you can do about it. When you buy a ticket, you have no legal guarantee that the train will run on time (or even at all), or that you'll have a seat when it does come. All this is explained in the small print, known as the conditions of carriage, which can be checked at station ticket offices.

Under the Train Operators' Charters you may be offered a small amount of compensation if you're stuck on a train that has been seriously delayed, for one hour or more, or if you have a season ticket for a train service that has been below the standard set for punctuality or reliability.

If you have a complaint about a train service, you can ask for a complaints form at a station or write to the customer relations manager for the route you have travelled on.

Cars & motorbikes

Getting started

The licence

It is an offence to drive a car or ride a motor cycle without the correct licence. You get a full driving licence when you have passed your test, and the licence will be valid until you are 70. Licences for drivers over 70 are issued for three years at a time.

New licences are now the size of a credit card and contain the holder's photograph. If you already hold a paper licence, you do not need to change it to the new format.

If you want to learn to drive, you need a provisional driving licence. Application forms are available from post offices. When you get your licence, sign it immediately - don't drive until you have done so. Car drivers can hold the same provisional licence until they are 70. A motorcyclist's provisional licence is only valid for two years, and cannot be renewed for a further twelve months after this.

Learning to drive a car

When you are driving on a provisional licence you must display `L' plates ('D' plates in Wales), which should be removed or covered up when the vehicle is not being

driven by a learner. You must not drive on a motorway, and you must have someone with you in the front passenger seat of the car who is over 21 and has held a full driving licence for at least three years. This person must be fit to drive and must not have had more than the legal amount of alcohol.

The driving test is in two parts, a written theory exam and a practical test. The theory paper, which must be passed before taking the practical test, lasts 40 minutes and is made up of 35 multiple-choice questions. It may be taken on a weekday, evening or Saturday at one of the 140 centres throughout the country.

Learning to drive a motorcycle

Motorcyclists also have to take a written theory paper and a practical test to gain a licence, unless they already have a full car licence, when only the practical test is required. Before you can ride a motorcycle on the road, you must successfully complete a Compulsory Basic Training course, unless you already have a full car licence and only want to drive a moped (with an engine of up to 50cc and a maximum speed of no more than 30mph).

Motorcyclists must learn to ride on machines no larger than 125cc. After passing the practical test, they are restricted for two years to bikes with a power output of up to 25 kw or 33 bhp, after which they may ride any size of bike. Riders over the age of 21 who don't want to wait this long to ride a larger bike can choose to take further tests, known as *direct* and *accelerated access*. See **Contacts** for information.

Like car drivers, learner motorcyclists may not ride on a motorway, nor may they carry a pillion passenger, unless the passenger is licensed to ride the particular type of machine that they are on.

MOT

Most vehicles which are three or more years old must pass the MOT test if they are to be used on the road.

Road tax

A car or motorbike must display a current tax disc, whether it is being used or just standing on the road. The fine for breaking this regulation is normally about twice the cost of the disc. The Driving and Vehicle Licensing Agency (usually known as the DVLA), now have powers to wheelclamp and remove vehicles not showing a current disc, and to charge a fee for their release. It is a crime to use a tax disc belonging to another vehicle. Vehicles manufactured before 1 January 1973 do not need a road tax disc. If you have a vehicle that you take off the road (eg for repairs) and decide not to tax, you must inform the DVLA on the reminder form sent to you when the vehicle licence is due for renewal. The penalty for not doing this is a fine of up to £1,000.

Insurance

It is an offence to drive, ride or even place a motor vehicle on the road without insurance. The penalties for this are very heavy, and it makes no difference for someone to say it was a genuine mistake and that they thought they were insured. Failure to have insurance means a fine and penalty points on a licence, and possible disqualification.

It is also an offence for someone to allow their car or motorcycle to be used by a person who is not insured to drive it.

There are three different kinds of motor insurance, offering different levels of cover:

● *third party insurance* only pays for damage caused to other people or their property (and not to your own vehicle). This is the minimum level of insurance cover required by law;

● *third party fire and theft* gives you further protection by covering your vehicle against theft or fire damage;

● *fully comprehensive insurance* is usually the most expensive, but covers the cost of accident repair damage to your vehicle as well as compensating you and others for injuries or damage in the accident.

When you apply for any insurance, make sure the information you give is accurate and complete. If it's not, your insurance will be invalid. It's an offence knowingly to make a false statement to obtain insurance. For more information, see **Money**, page 56.

Sarah bought a Morgan sports car, and insured it for her and her fiancé to drive. The car, worth £26,000 was stolen. When she claimed on her insurance, it came to light that her fiancé had received a serious motoring conviction several years ago, which Sarah had failed to mention on the application form. The insurance policy was therefore not valid, and Sarah received no compensation for the loss of her car.

Cars & motorbikes

At what age?

14 At 14 you can ride an electrically powered cycle.

At 16 you can ride a moped up to 50ccs, a small tractor, mowing machine or invalid car. If you receive a mobility allowance you can also drive a car. **16**

17 At 17 you can drive a car with up to 8 seats, a motorcycle, a large tractor and a van or lorry up to 3.5 tons.

At 18 you can drive a van or lorry up to 7.5 tons. **18**

21 At 21 you can drive all other vehicles. For hiring a car, most car hire companies have a minimum age of 21 or 23.

Happy Birthday

Buying a car

● A small popular car is usually less of a risk. Spare parts are cheaper and easier to obtain, insurance costs lower and it will probably be easier to sell when you want to change it.

● A car bought privately is usually cheaper than one bought from a dealer, but you have fewer rights if things go wrong. A person buying from a dealer is protected by the *Sale of Goods Act 1979* (see Money, page 48), whereas a car bought privately need only be "as described". The legal expression "caveat emptor" (meaning "buyer beware"), particularly applies when buying a second-hand car. It is notoriously difficult to get problems sorted out once you have paid for the car.

● Look at the car in daylight. Take

Traffic offences

Every vehicle on the road must meet a whole set of regulations covering brakes, tyres, lights, mirrors, steering and even windscreen washer bottles (which must, by law, never be empty). A police officer may stop a vehicle at any time to check that it is in roadworthy condition, and it is no excuse for the driver to claim that they didn't realise a light wasn't working. These are *absolute* offences and apply even if the driver was completely unaware of the problem.

  If the police believe a vehicle is unroadworthy, they can instruct the driver to get it checked and repaired by a garage (usually within 14 days), give the driver an on the spot fine or call up a specially trained vehicle examiner to inspect the car or bike there and then. A police officer who feels a vehicle is so dangerous that someone will probably be injured if it is used any further, can immediately ban it from being driven.

someone along with you who knows about cars. Check the owner's purchase documents to see if any hire-purchase payments are still due. For between £100-£300 the RAC, AA or Green Flag will inspect and report on the mechanical state of the car, check on the H Ppayments and tell you whether the car has been stolen or is an insurance write-off. HPI Autodata or AA Car Data provide a similar service at a slightly lower cost,without the mechanical inspection.

● Look to see if the car's mileage tallies with the MOT certificate and the service history. You can also check with previous owners. Ask the dealer if they have tried to verify the mileage - they have to do this by law. Be wary if there is a sticker on the speedometer indicating that there is no guarantee that the mileage is accurate.

● Ask to see the Vehicle Registration Document (V5). If it's a private sale, it should contain the seller's name and address. It also gives the Vehicle Identification Number (VIN), which should correspond with the number stamped on identification plates under the bonnet and on the floor. If you have any doubts, leave the car alone.

Anna went to look at a Ford Escort, advertised privately in her local paper. She asked the seller if the car had been in an accident. He said no, but having bought the car, Anna later found evidence of major crash repairs. She went back to the seller, pointed out the car was not as described and eventually got her money back. However, if the car had just been unreliable (even breaking down on her first drive), there is probably little she could have done, as there is nothing in law that states that a car bought privately must be of satisfactory or reasonable quality.

Cycling

Cyclists are expected to follow the same basic laws as other road users. They have a duty of care to pedestrians, other riders and road users. It is an offence, under the Highways Act 1835, to ride a bicycle (or tricycle) on the pavement - a law that applies to riders of all ages. It is also against the law to wheel a bike past a red traffic light or to ride it across a zebra crossing.

It is an offence to ride under the influence of alcohol or drugs. There is no breath test for cyclists; a court would instead be guided by evidence from the officer who made the arrest.

Driving

Safety

Seat belts and crash helmets

Where they are fitted, seat belts must now be worn by drivers and front and rear seat passengers. If a passenger in your car does not wear a belt, it is he or she who will be prosecuted, not you - unless the passenger is under 14, when it is your responsibility to see that a seat belt is worn.

If you are injured in an accident and were not wearing a seat belt, a court today will probably judge that you have contributed to your own injuries, and any compensation that you might be awarded will be significantly reduced.

Motorcyclist and pillion passengers must both wear an approved safety helmet on all journeys. This regulation does not apply to a follower of the Sikh religion while he is wearing a turban.

Speed limits

Car and motorcycles are limited to

30 30 mph in built-up areas, unless shown otherwise,

60 mph on single carriageways, **60**

70 70 mph on dual carriageways and motorways.

Speed limits are lower for buses, lorries and cars towing caravans.

Speeding

Speeding is an *absolute* offence, which means that it is no defence to say that you were not causing any danger by driving so fast, or that you didn't realise that you were breaking the speed limit. Nor is there much point in denying that you were travelling at the speed the police say you were, unless you can prove it. Courts are usually more inclined to believe the word of a police officer than a motorist accused of speeding.

If you break the speed limit, or are seen by the police to be driving carelessly or dangerously, you must be warned of the possibility of prosecution at the time of the offence or served with a summons within 14 days of the offence. Otherwise you cannot be convicted, unless an accident occurred at the time or immediately after.

Driving badly

If you are driving badly, especially if this leads to an accident, you may be charged with one of two offences.

Careless driving is to drive in a way that is not how a careful and reasonable driver would behave. Pulling out from a side road without looking is an example of this.

Dangerous driving is to drive in a way that is dangerous to people or property, such as driving very fast through a built-up area or overtaking on a sharp bend. Dangerous driving and causing death by dangerous driving are very serious offences, which courts will punish with fines, disqualification and imprisonment. If you face such a charge, get in touch with a solicitor straightaway.

Peter was involved in a crash with a motor cycle. He feared that it was his fault and that he would lose his licence, as he already had a number of penalty points. He persuaded his wife Sophie, who was not in the car at the time, to tell the police that it was she who was driving. A week later they both admitted the deception, but were charged with perverting the course of justice. Peter and Sophie were sentenced to four and two months in prison.

Drinking and driving

Alcohol seriously affects a driver's judgement and reactions. There is no law that limits a driver to a certain number of drinks, such as two pints of beer or one glass of wine, but there is a maximum amount of alcohol that you may have in your body while driving or being in charge of a car. In law, being in charge of a car includes simply sitting in the driving seat of parked car.

The limits

The amount of alcohol in a person's body can be measured in their breath, blood or urine. A driver will be found guilty of drink-driving if they have more than 35 micrograms of alcohol in 100 ml of breath, 80 mg of alcohol in 100 ml of blood, or more than 107 mg of alcohol in 100 ml of urine. In 1999 or 2000, it is likely that the amount of alcohol that a driver may consume will be further reduced.

Breath tests

The police will carry out a roadside breath test to check whether a driver has more than the permitted amount of alcohol in their body. The police can breathalyse anyone whom they reasonably suspect of driving with excess alcohol, who is committing a moving traffic offence, or has been involved in a road accident, however minor, even if there is no suspicion of alcohol. A uniformed police officer is also quite entitled to stop motorists at random in order to see whether there is a reasonable suspicion that they have consumed any alcohol. If there is, the officer can go on to ask the motorist to take a breath test. If the test is positive, the driver will be arrested and taken to a police station for further breath tests or, in some circumstances, a blood or urine test.

No escape

A driver who fails to blow into the device properly, or refuses to take a test, will still end up with a heavy fine and have his or her licence *endorsed* with three or four penalty points. Courts rarely accept that there are special reasons for drivers being over the limit. Disqualification from driving is almost automatic. A drunken driver who causes someone's death may be sent to prison for up to ten years, and will be disqualified from driving for at least two years.

Paul had had a few drinks when he was phoned by a friend who had run out of petrol, miles from anywhere, with his old and sick mother. Paul got into his car to go and fetch them, but was stopped by the police and breathalysed positive. Although he told the court that it was an emergency, the magistrates still found Paul guilty of drinking and driving, saying that the police, RAC or AA could instead have been called to help.

Penalty points

Courts deal with most motoring offences through a system of penalty points which are entered on a driver's licence. Anyone receiving twelve or more points within a period of three years will almost always be disqualified from driving for at least six months. Details of the points carried for each offence are given in the Highway Code. Drivers who have six or more penalty points on their licence within two years of their test, go back to being a learner until they pass a further test.

Accidents

What to do

Accidents happen to the most careful of drivers, often through no fault of their own. If you are involved in an accident, there are certain things that you should and should not do....

- **Stop immediately. Try to stay calm, even if people are yelling and screaming at you.**
- **Check that everyone involved in the accident is OK. If anyone is injured, call an ambulance before you do anything else.**
- **You must give your name and address and details of your vehicle to anyone who has reasonable need to know them. This includes a police officer at the scene of the accident, anyone who is injured, anyone whose property is damaged and the owner of any animal injured or killed. (This applies to horses, cows, sheep, goats and dogs - but not cats.) If someone is injured, you must also produce your insurance certificate to show that you are properly insured. If you can't do this at the time of the accident, then you must give this information to the police as soon as possible, and certainly within 24 hours. If you don't, you will be committing an offence.**
- **Make sure you get the name, address, vehicle registration number and insurance details of the other drivers involved.**
- **Contact your insurance company as soon as possible, and also make a detailed note of everything that happened. This should cover the time of day, weather, light, estimated speeds, position of vehicles before and after the accident, what**

people said and anything else that you think might be relevant. If you can, take photos before anything is moved, or draw a sketch plan as soon as you feel able to do so.
- **Don't drive away without stopping. It is a criminal offence.**
- **Be cautious if the other driver suggests not calling the police and offers you cash to cover the damage. It might be an offence not to report the accident, and you may find that the damage to your vehicle costs a lot more than you are being offered.**
- **Don't admit it was your fault. You may find later that the other driver was drunk, driving too fast, or without lights - in which case you might not be to blame at all. If you do admit responsibility, your words may end up by being used against you in court and may affect your insurance claim.**

Stolen vehicles

Stealing a vehicle to sell on to someone else is theft. Joy-riding, or taking a car to ride around in and then dumping it, is a different offence known as "taking a vehicle without the owner's consent". Both are punishable by a fine or im-prisonment. The Aggravated Vehicle-Taking Act 1992 gives courts powers to deal with joy-riders who drive dangerously and are involved in an accident causing injury and damage. A sentence of up to five years' imprisonmen may be imposed, with a year's automatic disqualification from driving.

If you buy a car that turns out to be stolen, it remains the property of the true owner - meaning that you will almost certainly lose your money, unless you can get it back from the person from whom you bought the car.

CONTACTS See PAGES 119-127 for organisations able to give help & advice

POLICE
& COURTS

102 POWERS & DUTIES

102 STOP & SEARCH

104 ARREST

106 CHARGE CAUTION RELEASE

108 IN COURT

young citizen's **passport**

Police

Powers & duties

Most of the information that the police receive comes from the general public. Without this help they could do very little.

Much of the law setting out police powers and duties when investigating crime is contained in the *Police and Criminal Evidence Act 1984*. As part of this, the government publishes guidelines which the police must follow when searching for and collecting evidence. These are known as the *Codes of Practice*. If they are broken when the police are, say, questioning a suspect, a judge or magistrate may decide that the evidence obtained cannot be used in court, and the police officers concerned may be disciplined.

Copies of the Codes of Practice are available from libraries and at every police station. Anyone questioned by the police has a right to read them.

Police discipline

Police officers must obey both the law of the land, and their own code of discipline. This discipline code is broken if an officer.....

- **neglects their duty, without good reason;**
- **makes a false written or spoken statement;**
- **misuses their authority, eg through unnecessary violence;**
- **is rude or abusive to members of the public;**
- **is in any way racially discriminatory in their behaviour.**

Stop!

If a police officer stops you in the street, you are entitled to know the officer's name and the police station where they work. You are also entitled to know why the officer has stopped you. It is not acceptable for this to be simply because of your colour, dress, hairstyle or the fact that you might have been in trouble before.

Strictly speaking, you don't have to answer a police officer's questions, but someone who refuses to give their name and address may well find themselves arrested if the officer believes that they have something to hide.

However, if the police suspect that you have committed (or are about to commit) an arrestable offence - such as theft, assault or carrying an offensive weapon - then you must give your name and address, but need not say any more. You have the right not to answer any more questions until you have received legal advice (see below).

Stay calm 1 If you're stopped by the police, keep calm and don't overreact. If you're obstructive and rude, you're more likely to be arrested. Staying calm will also help you remember what happened and what was said. If you deliberately mislead the police by giving false information or wasting their time, you risk a fine or even imprisonment.

Search!

People The police do not have the power to search anyone they choose, but they can search someone (and the vehicle in which they are travelling), who has been arrested or is suspected of carrying...

● **illegal drugs;**
● **stolen goods or goods on which duty has not been paid;**
● **weapons, or anything that might be used as a weapon; or**
● **anything that might be used for theft, burglary, deception, joyriding or the hunting or poaching of animals.**

Any search involving more than a check of your outer clothing should be done out of public view or in a police station or van. If the search requires more than the removal of outer clothing, it should be done by someone of the same sex. The way the search is carried out can depend on what the police are looking for. For example, the police may decide to make an intimate search of someone suspected of carrying drugs - given the possibility that the drugs are being hidden inside the person's body.

Stay calm 2 If you, or the vehicle in which you are travelling, are searched by the police, the officer should state beforehand why the search is taking place and what they expect to find. You have every right to ask for an explanation if this has not been made clear.

If the police search you illegally, they are committing an assault. But if they have good reason, and you refuse, you may be charged with obstruction.

The police should make a written record of the search. You can ask for a copy at any time within the next year.

Special powers Police powers of search in certain circumstances have been extended by the *Criminal Justice and Public Order Act 1994*. If a senior police officer believes that a serious violent incident might take place in the area, they can give officers the authority to stop any person or vehicle to search for offensive weapons or dangerous instruments. This applies even when the constable has no reasonable grounds for suspecting that the person stopped might have broken the law.

If you are stopped in this way, you are entitled to a written record of the search.

Failing to stop, when asked by a police officer, can result in a fine or even imprisonment.

Under the Crime and Disorder Act 1998, the police may also, with the authority of an officer of the rank of inspector or above, remove and seize anything covering a person's face if the officer believes it is being used to hide their identity, and that there is a risk of serious violence in the area.

Police

Property

The police do not have the power to enter and search any house or building that they choose. But they are allowed to carry out a search if....

● **they have the agreement of the occupier of the building; or**
● **they have reason to believe they might find someone who has committed an arrestable offence, or to look for evidence in a property that was occupied by someone before they were arrested; or**
● **they have a warrant (or permission) from a court; or**
● **in order to catch an escaped prisoner, save life, prevent serious property damage or to prevent some kind of disturbance.**

If possible, the police should explain why they are making the search and should keep a record of whether they needed to use force to get in, any damage caused, and anything they took away. If the search proves to be unlawful, it may be possible to get compensation, but this will not be easy.

Arrest

When the police make an arrest, they are taking the person under the care and control of the law. This means that for the time being, the suspect loses certain freedoms - such as to go and do as they please - but, in return, has certain rights designed to protect them from unreasonable treatment.

If you are arrested and taken to a police station, you are entitled to .....

● **know the reason for your arrest;**
● **see a solicitor (see below); have someone told where you are;**
● **read a copy of the Codes of Practice, which explain the procedures the police should follow when questioning you (see page 102).**

Helping the police with their enquiries

If you are asked to go to a police station to help with enquiries, it's important to know if you are being arrested, or whether the decision to attend is up to you. If you are being asked to go voluntarily, you may refuse - although the police may then decide to arrest you - and then you have to go.

You are entitled to send a message to your family or a friend telling them where you are, and to receive free legal advice from a solicitor, even though you are attending the police station voluntarily.

If you have not been arrested and go to the police station voluntarily, you may leave at any time you wish.

CITIZENSHIP FOUNDATION

You should be given a written note of these rights and cautioned. For the wording of this, see page 106.

You can be held by the police if they do not have enough evidence to charge you, but have good reason to believe that they can obtain further evidence by continuing with your detention.

You cannot normally be held for more than 24 hours without being charged or released. If a serious offence is being investigated, a senior police officer can authorise your detention for a further 12 hours, which can be extended up to a total of 96 hours, but only with the approval of a magistrates' court.

Questioning

If you are under 17, the police should not normally interview you without your parent or an "appropriate adult" present. An appropriate adult is someone who knows you, such as an adult friend or teacher.

You must give the police your name and address, but you have the right after that to stay silent and not answer any further questions. However, the court will be told of this if the case goes to trial, and it may strengthen the case against you. If you refuse to answer questions in court, the magistrates or jury are allowed to take this into account in deciding whether you are guilty.

There are clear rules governing the way a police officer can question a person, which are designed to stop unfair pressure being placed on a suspect. There should be regular breaks for food, the cell and interview room should be clean and properly heated, and the police should not follow a line of questioning that puts unreasonable pressure on the suspect. Someone who is deaf or has difficulty in understanding English should be given a signer or an interpreter.

If, after questioning, the police decide to arrest you, they should give you written information about your legal rights.

Tape recording Your interview at the police station will probably be recorded on tape. It will begin with questions about your name and address before moving on to more serious matters.

If your interview is not recorded, notes should be made by the officer concerned. You should have the opportunity to see these notes and to sign them if you agree that they are a fair record of what was said.

Police

Fingerprints & photographs

The police can take fingerprints of anyone over the age of ten who they have reason to believe has been involved in a crime. If the person doesn't consent, reasonable force can be used. The police are also allowed to photograph anyone charged with a recordable offence, but cannot use force if the suspect refuses. Fingerprints and photographs must be destroyed if the person is charged and found not guilty, or not charged at all.

The caution

Once a police officer has reason to believe that you have committed an offence, they must caution you by saying that you do not have to say anything, but that it may harm your defence if you do not mention when questioned something which you later rely on in court. Anything you do say may be given in evidence.

Legal advice

In almost all circumstances, anyone who has been arrested, or who goes to a police station voluntarily, is entitled to legal advice from a solicitor. The consultation with the solicitor is free and in private.

If you have been arrested or are being questioned about a serious arrestable offence, or if you feel at all unsure about your legal position, it is better not to answer questions (except your name and address) until you have had a chance to speak to a solicitor.

If the police are investigating a very serious offence they can, with the approval of a senior officer, delay access to a solicitor on the grounds that allowing the suspect to talk to a solicitor might interfere with the evidence, alert other suspects or hinder the recovery of stolen property.

Charge, caution, release

After questioning you, the police must decide what to do next. If there appears to be enough evidence, they can .....

● **charge you with the offence; or**
● **send the papers to the Crown Prosecution Service, for them to decide whether to charge you; or**
● **arrange to issue you with** *formal caution*. **This is a strong warning from a senior police officer reminding you that you could have been sent to court, and that if you commit further offences, that is almost certainly what will happen. Formal cautions are given more often now because the re-offence rate is lower amongst those who do not go to court. Cautions, however, are not for serious offences and can be given only if the accused admits guilt.**

If the police feel there is not enough evidence to make a charge, they will either decide to take no further action (and the case against you will be dropped) or will delay any decision while further enquiries are made.

A new approach

As part of the *Crime and Disorder Act 1998* the police are experimenting in certain areas with what is called a final warning scheme to replace the existing system of cautioning. It will apply only to young offenders (under 18) and not adults. A first offence will result in a young person being given a reprimand, a final warning or facing criminal charges, depending on the seriousness of the case. After a reprimand, a further offence will lead to a warning or charge. Someone who has received a warning and who offends again, will normally be charged.

Charged If you are to be charged, you will be given a charge sheet indicating the nature of the offence, when and where you are due to appear in court and the conditions of your bail.

Once you are charged you should not usually be asked any further questions unless, perhaps, new information has come to light.

Bail If you are charged with an offence, the law states that you should normally be released on bail - unless the police doubt the truth of the name and address that you have given, or believe you should be held for the protection of others, or feel that you are unlikely to turn up in court if released.

If the police do not release you, you must be brought before a magistrate at the earliest opportunity, who will decide whether you can be released on bail and, if so, what conditions should apply. For example, you may be required to report to the police station once a week, or to have someone provide a financial guarantee that you will be present in court when required.

A person who is charged with, or already convicted of, murder, attempted murder, manslaughter or rape will only be given bail in very exceptional circumstances. Courts also need not grant bail if it appears that the defendant was already on bail when the offence was committed.

Complaints against the police

If you feel that you have suffered, or witnessed police misconduct, you may decide that you want to make an official complaint. This should be done within one year of the incident.

Think about what happened, make sure you are clear what was wrong. If it is a serious matter, it's a good idea to speak to a solicitor or contact your local Citizens Advice Bureau beforehand.

You can make your complaint, in person, at your local police station or write to the Chief Constable of the police force concerned. The address will be in the phone book. In reply, you may get an apology, or an explanation of the officer's conduct.

If you are not satisfied with this, or your complaint is of a serious nature, there will be a full investigation by a senior officer of the force involved. Further information on this is available from the Police Complaints Authority, see Contacts.

The Crown Prosecution Service

The job of investigating a crime and charging a suspect is done by the police, but the decision as to whether to continue with the case and bring it to court is made by the Crown Prosecution Service (CPS). This is an independent prosecuting service, made up of trained lawyers, who decide whether there is a realistic chance of conviction and whether the seriousness of the crime merits a trial. If the answer to either of these questions is "no", the case will be dropped.

It is difficult to predict the amount of time it will take to investigate and bring a case to court. If you are charged with an offence normally heard in a magistrates' court, you should know within six months whether you are to be prosecuted.

Under the *Crime and Disorder Act 1998*, time limits will be set on the amount of time someone under 18 might have to wait between their arrest and appearance in court, or between their conviction and sentence. But these are unlikely to come in to force nationally until around 2001.

Courts

You will be told of the date and time of your appearance in court on the police charge sheet or by summons through the post.

If you are 17 or under, your case will normally be heard in a youth court. If you are 18 or over it will be held in the local adult magistrates' court.

Legal aid

Help with the cost of legal advice and the presentation of your case in court is called legal aid.

If you receive a summons to court, it is important to get legal advice as soon as possible. You may wish to use the solicitor that you saw at the police station, or you can consult another one - it's up to you. You should be able to have the cost of at least your first interview with a solicitor met by legal aid.

If you are to be tried in a magistrates' or a Crown Court, you may be able to get help with the cost of a solicitor, and possibly a barrister, to present your case in court. The amount you will be given will depend on your income, but you may be required to make a contribution towards the cost.

If you find yourself in court without anyone to give you advice, you can ask to see the duty solicitor or ask the magistrates to delay your case until you've had time to talk to someone. Help of this type is again free, but the magistrates will probably want to know why you did not sort it out earlier.

The Court Service

If you need to go to court, for example as a witness or juror, and need information on what you can expect or what you might have to do, your local court should be able to

help. (See Courts in the phone book.) Further details are given in the Courts' Charter, see **Contacts**.

Juries

The job of a jury, which sits in a Crown Court, is to decide on the facts of a criminal case and on the guilt or innocence of the accused. It is made up of twelve adults, aged between 18 - 70, who have lived in Britain for a continuous period of five years from the age of 13. They are chosen at random from the local Electoral Register (see **Government**), but there are certain categories of people who cannot be selected. These include judges, magistrates, solicitors, barristers, ministers of religion, prison, police and probation officers, anyone on bail or who has been on probation within the last five years, and anyone sentenced to prison, detention centre, youth custody or community service within the last ten years.

If you are called as a member of a jury, you will usually be given about six weeks' notice. Although some people, such as MPs, members of the armed forces and the medical profession have the right to be excused, normally it is compulsory. But if there is a strong reason why you are unable to serve - such as exams, a holiday which has been already booked, the care of a relative or major problems at work - then you can be excused, although it is important to make this clear as soon as possible.

Those called for jury service are given information about what they are expected to do, and are normally shown a short video about trial procedure before the case begins. They are also able to claim the cost of travel to Court and a small financial allowance.

Courts

Youth court

If the accused is under 18, the case will probably be heard in a youth court, although a young person charged with an adult will if be sent for trial at the magistrate's court or Crown Court, if the case is serious enough.

In exceptional cases, such as when a young person is charged with murder, the trial will be held in a Crown Court.

A youth court is made up of three magistrates, trained to deal with cases involving young people. At least one of the magistrates should be a man, and one a woman.

If the accused is under 16, their parents must attend the court. Parents of 16 or 17 year olds may also be ordered to attend.

Members of the public are not allowed in a youth court to listen to the case, nor can the name or identity of the young person accused be reported in the press.

Magistrates' court

All criminal cases pass through magistrates' courts, in some way or another. Normally three magistrates sit in court. Also known as justices of the peace, they are usually not lawyers, but members of the local community. Magistrates will reach a verdict themselves on all cases involving less serious offences (known as summary offences). More serious cases are dealt with by the Crown Court (with a jury), but before they reach this stage, it is the magistrates' job to decide whether there is enough evidence for the accused to stand trial. There are some offences that can be heard by either a magistrates' or Crown Court, and the accused can decide which to choose.

Crown Court

This is the court where more serious (called indictable) offences are heard. A judge takes charge of the hearing to make sure that the evidence is properly presented, but the verdict is reached by the jury. If the defendant is found guilty, the judge will pass sentence. In deciding on this, they take into account the circumstances surrounding the case, previous convictions, and possibly the background of the defendant if it is thought to have any bearing on the case.

Age of criminal responsibility

Normally a child under the age of ten who breaks the law is not charged with the crime. It's felt that, on the whole, children under this age are too young to weigh up what is right and wrong and deliberately break the law. However, children under ten who are out of control can be taken into care by a youth court.

Until recently, children aged between ten and thirteen were also treated as if they were incapable of crime, unless it could be shown that they knew what they were doing was seriously wrong. This has been abolished by the *Crime and Disorder Act 1998*.

Following another recent change in the law, boys under the age of fourteen may now be charged with sexual offences.

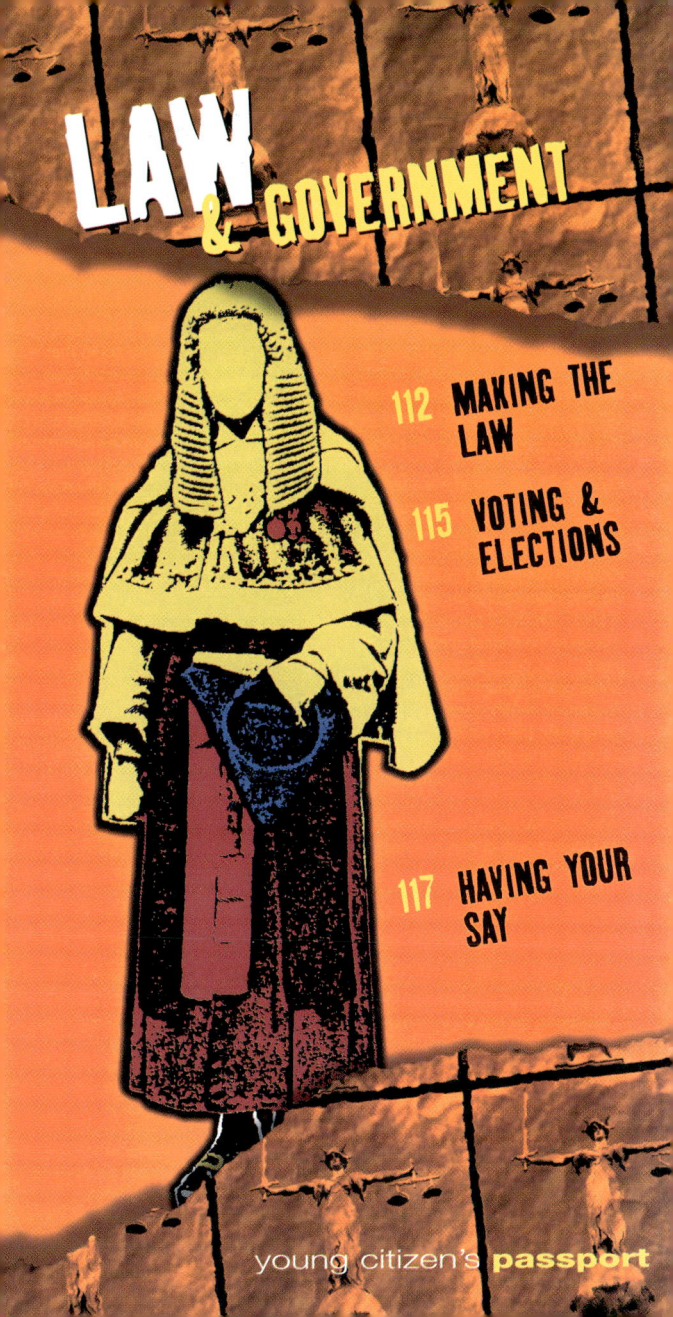

LAW & GOVERNMENT

112 MAKING THE LAW

115 VOTING & ELECTIONS

117 HAVING YOUR SAY

young citizen's **passport**

Making the law

Parliament

Between 50-60 major new laws are passed by Parliament each year. Starting as a Bill, each one must be debated and voted on by the House of Commons and the House of Lords before becoming law. The House of Lords can recommend changes and delay the progress of a Bill, but it can't actually stop it from being passed. The only Bill that the House of Lords can reject is one that tries to extend a Parliament's life beyond five years (the maximum time between general elections) - a protection against power being seized by a dictator. In 1999 or 2000, the Government intends to begin the long process of changing the House of Lords, which will probably include a change to the system of hereditary peers.

After going through both Houses of Parliament, a Bill becomes an Act by being given the royal assent by the Queen. Today this is a formality. The last monarch to refuse to approve an Act was Queen Anne in 1707.

Most Bills are put to Parliament by the Government as part of its overall policy, although a small number are presented by individual MPs and Peers. These are known as private members' Bills. Few of these become law, as there is only a limited amount of time to debate and vote on them. Most of Parliament's time is spent on Government business.

Courts

When a case comes to court, the magistrates or judge normally deal with it in the same way as courts have done in the past. This is called a system of precedent and ensures that similar cases are dealt with in a consistent way. However, there are times when the circumstances of a case have not arisen before, or when a judge decides that existing judgements do not reflect modern society. In these situations, by their decision, judges can create or change the law.

The National Assembly for Wales

Elections for the 60 members who will make up the Welsh Assembly take place in May 1999, and the Assembly will be established shortly after this. All laws for Wales will still be passed by Parliament in London, although the Assembly will debate and give its views on issues directly affecting Wales. It will also have responsibility for deciding how certain kinds of law, such as education, health, industry, agriculture, transport, training and environment, will be put into practice in Wales. Questions of foriegn affairs, defence, taxation, social security and broadcasting will be decided for the whole of the United Kingdom by the Government in London.

A month after separating from his wife, a man broke into her parents' house where she was staying, and tried to have sex with her against her will. The husband was found guilty of attempted rape and sentenced to five years imprisonment. He appealed on the grounds that a husband could not be found guilty of raping his wife. The case went to the Court of Appeal and then to the House of Lords, where it was heard by five senior judges. The judges decided that the ruling that a husband could not be found guilty of raping his wife (which went back to before 1736) should no longer form part of the law, since husband and wife were now seen as equal partners in marriage. As a result, the law changed and a man who forces his wife to have sexual intercourse against her will, may now be found guilty of rape.

European law

Britain is one of the 15 states that are members of the European Union (EU). Representatives of EU countries form the European Parliament, the European Commission and the Council of Ministers - and it is these bodies which are responsible for creating new laws. European law comes to us in two main forms - as *regulations* and *directives*. Regulations apply to every member state and, as soon as they have been issued, automatically become law in this country. Directives indicate what the law should be, and each country must bring in its own law putting the directive into practice. European law covers much, but not all of our life, concentrating in particular on agriculture, transport, the environment, sex discrimination and civil liberties. It does not tend to get involved in questions of criminal justice, education or property rights.

Mrs Day, who worked 11 hours a week part-time as a cleaner, did not receive any redundancy pay when she was made redundant by Hertfordshire County Council. This was because, under English law, redundancy pay was available only to those working for 16 or more hours a week. Mrs Day thought this was unfair and, with help from the Equal Opportunities Commission, took her case to Court. Three senior judges listened to the evidence and decided that, by denying employment protection rights to part-time workers, English law was discriminating against women, who made up the bulk of the part-time workforce. The judges said that this broke an important principle of European law, which says that men and women should be treated equally. As a result, English law was soon changed by Parliament giving employment protection rights to all UK workers, whether full or part-time.

Making the law

European Convention on Human Rights

This list of human rights was drawn up to provide protection for people after the horrors of the Second World War. It took effect from 1953 and sets out fundamental rights and freedoms that is felt everybody should have. These include a right to liberty, a right to a fair trial, freedom of thought, conscience and religion etc..

Anyone, who feels that their rights under the Convention have been broken, may take their case to the European Court of Human Rights in Strasbourg. It is a slow and complicated process and many conditions are attached. One of these is that the person must have first used all possible means within their own country to settle their complaint before applying to the Court. Efforts will be made to reach an agreed settlement, but if this is not possible, the Court will hear the case and deliver its verdict. If it finds that the Convention has been broken, it can award damages and costs to a successful applicant and governments must comply with decisions that go against them.

Unlike most other European countries, Britain has not, until recently, incorporated the European Convention into its own law. This will change under the *Human Rights Act 1998.* When the Act comes into force, around the year 2000, all new law must be in line with the Convention and existing law will have to be interpreted by the courts in accordance with it.

In September 1976 Jeffrey, aged 16, took a short cut home from his school in Scotland through a nearby cemetry. This was against school rules and Jeffrey was reported to the head, who decided that he should be punished with the strap. The boy refused. He was supported by his parents who said that they thought corporal punishment was morally wrong. Jeffrey was suspended.

Both the school and the local authority suggested various ways in which he might be allowed back - but could not promise that Jeffrey would never be beaten for misbehaviour. Jeffrey's parents would not agree to this. They claimed that the local authority were breaking part of the European Convention on Human Rights which says that no one shall be denied the right to education and that parents have the right to make sure that their children are taught in a way that respects their religious and philosophical beliefs.

When the case eventually reached the European Court of Human Rights in 1982, the Court agreed with Jeffrey's mother, who had made the application.

As a result, the British government had to change the law on corporal punishment in schools. This took some time to achieve, but corporal punishment was eventually largely abolished in schools in the UK in 1987.

Voting & elections

Who can vote?

You must be 18 or over on the day of the election and your name must be on the Electoral Register. For Westminster elections, you must be a citizen of the United Kingdom, the Commonwealth or of the Irish Republic, and live in this country. For European and local elections, nationals of the EU states living in the UK may also vote.

Who can't vote?

Those unable to vote in Parliamentary elections include most people compulsorily held for treatment for mental illness (although the rights of people in this category are not absolutely clear), most people serving a prison sentence, anyone convicted of corrupt practices at an election during the previous five years and members of the House of Lords.

Registering to vote

Each year, an electoral registration form is delivered to every household in the country. The form should be completed with details of everyone living there, aged 16 and over. Registering to vote is not linked in any way to paying taxes, but it is technically an offence knowingly to fail to put yourself on the Electoral Register.

If you move away for work or college or are on holiday, you can get a postal vote, provided that you are on the Electoral Register. There are also special arrangements for people, such as the registered blind, who cannot get to the polling station on the day.

You can check if your name is on the Register of Electors at your local main library or council offices.

Councillor, MP or MEP?

You can stand for political office from the age of 21. If you want to be a local councillor you must either...

- have your name on the local electoral register; or
- rent or own land or property or have worked in the area for the last twelve months; or
- have lived in, or within three miles of, the area for the last twelve months.

These rules do not apply to MPs or MEPs. Candidates standing as an MP must pay a deposit of £500, which they lose if they get less than 5% of the votes cast. The deposit for MEPs is £1,000, likely to go up to £5,000 for the 1999 elections.

Voting & elections

Local elections

The election of local councillors is held every four years, usually in the first week of May, although not all councils hold them in the same year.

In most areas there are three levels of local government - county, district or town, and community or parish councils. In London the local councils are the 32 Boroughs. In other major cities, it is usually the metropolitan districts and unitary authorities that carry out most of the important local government work.

Between them, and sometimes together with national government, these councils are responsible for education, planning, refuse, environment, recreation, passenger transport, libraries, children's homes, council housing and car parks.

As well as deciding how the services are to be run, local councillors also take up problems on behalf of those living in their area.

General elections

The election of all 659 MPs must take place at least every five years. Often, however, the party in power will call an election before this if it feels it will help its chances of gaining another term of office or, more rarely, because it has been defeated on a vital vote in the House of Commons and has lost the confidence of the House.

Most MPs represent a political party and each represents a defined area, called a constituency. The party with the greatest number of MPs will form the government, with the party leader becoming Prime Minister. If an MP dies or resigns, a by-election will take place to elect a new MP for their constituency.

Even if not a member of the Government, your MP can have influence by speaking in debates, talking to ministers and other MPs, and by trying to get a private member's Bill made law. An MP represents everyone in their constituency.

There is the possibility that our voting system will be changed to one of proportional representation. The Government has said that it plans to hold a referendum on this.

European elections

At European Elections we elect members of the European Parliament which meets both in Strasbourg (France) and Brussels (Belgium). These take place every five years. Most candidates belong to one of the main political parties and, if elected, join the MEPs of the 14 other countries in the European Union.

MEPs help to make European law, by examining and commenting on proposals made by the European Commission (see page 113). Their ability to influence EU legislation and finance has grown considerably since the first elected Parliament in 1979.

Having your say

If you feel strongly about something and want to get involved yourself, a library, Citizens Advice Bureau, or one of the organisations listed in the Contacts section can probably give you some of information you need.

Campaigning

This ranges from individual action to something more co-ordinated, as a member of a group. Letter writing is the usual starting point - do your research, send it to a named person (the most senior within the organisation), keep a copy, and try to get others involved as well. If you can get a letter published in a newspaper, many more will know about your views, but do give your name and address - although you can ask the paper not to publish it.

Writing to your councillor, MP or MEP

If your problem is local, contact your local councillor through the council office. MPs or MEPs can best take up problems for which the Government or European Union are responsible. Most MPs and some MEPs have local 'surgeries' for which no appointment is necessary. They are often on a Saturday, and advertised in the local paper. You can also write to your MEP locally and your MP at the House of Commons. Addresses are obtainable from your local library, and should also be under Member of Parliament in the business section of the phone book.

Protest

The same laws apply to people taking part in political action as any other area of life. Criminal damage, theft, assault etc. remain crimes - no matter how good the cause.

Demonstrations and marches are controlled by the *Public Order Act 1986* and the *Criminal Justice and Public Order Act 1994*. Organisers must inform the local police where and when the march will take place and how many people will be involved. If the police believe the demonstration is likely to disrupt seriously the life of the community, a senior police officer can issue a ban for a period of up to three months.

Having your say

Hunt saboteurs

The *Criminal Justice and Public Order Act 1994* introduced the offence of aggravated trespass. It was aimed at hunt saboteurs, but can affect anyone who causes disruption to people going about their lawful business. It is an offence to trespass on private land in order to intimidate, obstruct or disrupt people (such as trying to distract the hounds by blowing horns), who are doing a lawful activity.

Complaining

If you have a complaint about something you have bought or a service you have received, it's important to act quickly. Some companies and many public services have special procedures for dealing with complaints. If it's a public service, such as a hospital or benefits agency, ask to see a copy of their charter which shows the level of service you are entitled to expect. If your complaint is not dealt with properly, think about contacting your local councillor or MP, particularly if your problem is over a public service.

Whoever you are dealing with, it will be more effective if you......

● act as quickly as possible,

● think carefully about what you want to achieve and if necessary get advice;

● make sure you talk or write directly to a person - such as the manager or director of services - who has the authority to deal with your complaint;

● always find out the name of the person who you are talking to;

● keep a record of phone calls or letters that you send;

● stick to the facts, and work out how the law can help you;

● state clearly what you want to be  done, set a reasonable time within which this should happen, and get back in touch if they haven't met the deadline.

If you are still unhappy with the way your problem has been handled, you may be able to take your case to an Ombudsman. See **Contacts**.

Judicial review

If a public body - like a government department, local authority or hospital - makes a decision which actually seems to be against the law, you can apply to have that decision reviewed in the High Court. Known as judicial review, it's a way of having illegal or unreasonable decisions changed. Examples of this have been when people have challenged a ruling by the Home Office to deport someone who is a British citizen, or when they have questioned a hospital's right to withhold an operation in a genuinely urgent case.

A judicial review can be started only when all other avenues of complaint have been exhausted. It's a very complicated process and so, before doing anything, it's important to get advice from a solicitor who understands this area of law.

Charter Marks

If you feel that a public service is doing a very good job, you can nominate them for a *Charter Mark Award*. Winners can use the Charter Mark in their publicity for three years. See **Contacts** for further details.

CONTACTS   See PAGES 119-127 for organisations able to give help & advice

Getting information & advice

● Before you write, phone or ask for information, think carefully about exactly what you need to know. Don't be overlong in your explanation, keep to the most important details.

● If you are telephoning, you will probably first speak to a receptionist who may not be able to answer your question. Explain that you'd like to talk to someone about ....(name the subject), and you should be put through. If they can't help, they may be able to give you the name of someone who can.

● It sometimes helps to put a few key words down on paper to remind you of what you want to say. You'll also need a pen and paper to make notes of what you are told.

● It's a good idea to ask who you are talking to so, if you write or phone again, you can give the name of the person you first spoke to.

The following names and addresses are arranged according to the chapters in the main part of the book and are just a few of the many organisations that exist to help with the whole range of law-related problems.

General

Childline, Freepost 1111, London N1 0BR. A free 24 hr. helpline for any child in danger or distress, tel 0800 1111.

Children's Legal Centre, University of Essex, Wivenhoe Park, Colchester, Essex CO4 3SQ, offers advice on a wide range of issues by letter and phone. The advice line is open every weekday afternoon, 2pm-5pm, and Wed morning, 10am-12 noon, tel 01206 873 820.

Citizens Advice Bureau, usually known as the CAB, gives free, confidential and independent information and advice on all kinds of problems. You can enquire by phone or at one of their offices, found in most towns and cities. For your nearest CAB, see the local phone book.

Disability Law Services, Part 2nd Floor North, High Holborn House, High Holborn, London WC1V 6RL, tel 0171 831 8031. Able to advise and help disabled people, their family, friends and carers on a wide range of law-related subjects including work, housing, benefits and community care.

Free Representation Unit, Peer House, 4th Floor, 8-14 Verulam Street WC1X 8LZ, tel 0171 831 0692. A charitable organisation of barristers and law students who will represent clients without charge at social security and industrial tribunals - but they will only take cases referred to them by solicitors, law centres and CABs.

Information Shops are specifically designed for young people and organised by the National Youth Agency, with trained workers able to provide information and support.   For the address and phone number of your nearest Information Shop, contact the National Youth Agency, 17-23 Albion Street, Leicester LE1 6GD, tel 01162 856 789.

Law Centres Federation, Duchess House, 18-19 Warren Street, London W1P 5DB, tel 0171 387 8570, can give you the name and address of your nearest law centre.

Law Society, 113 Chancery Lane, London WC2A 1PL, tel 0171 242 1222, provides information on using a solicitor. If you wish to make a complaint about a solicitor, contact the Office for the Supervision of Solicitors, Victoria Ct., 8 Dormer Place, Leamington Spa, Warwickshire, CV32 5AE, tel 01926 820 082.

Legal Aid Board, head office, 85 Gray's Inn Road, London WC1X 8AA, tel 0171 813 1000. Information leaflets available on applying for legal aid.

Liberty, 21 Tabbard Street, London SE1 4LA, tel 0171 403 3888. Liberty in a campaigning organisation able to answer questions by post from people who feel their civil liberties have been infringed.

The Ombudsman If you have a problem with a local or national government department, the health service, an insurance company, a bank or building society or a legal service and are not happy with how your complaint has been dealt with, you can refer your case to an Ombudsman. You must first, however, have done everything you can to sort things out yourself with the person or organisation concerned. Your local CAB can explain how to submit a complaint, or you can write to the appropriate office at one of the addresses below. If the Ombudsman decides your complaint is reasonable, the department or organisation responsible will be asked to do something about it - which might mean that you get an apology or compensation. New procedures may also be put into place to make sure the same thing doesn't happen again.

The Local Government Ombudsman (for England), 21 Queen Anne's Gate, London SW1H 9BU, tel 0171 915 3210, and (for Wales), Derwen House, Court Road, Bridgend CF31 1BN, tel 01656 661 325; the **Health Service Ombudsman**, 11th Floor, Millbank Tower, London SW1P 4QP, tel 0171 217 4051, and (for Wales), 5th Floor, Capital Tower, Greyfriars Road, Cardiff CF1 3AG, tel 01222 394 621; the **Insurance Ombudsman Bureau**, City Gate One, 135 Park Street, London SE1 9EA, tel 0171 928 4488; the **Banking Ombudsman**, 70 Gray's Inn Road, London WC1X 8NB, tel 0171 404 9944; the **Legal Services Ombudsman**, 22 Oxford Court, Oxford Street, Manchester M2 3WQ, tel 0161 236 9532.

Service First For a list of national charters, call the Service First publications line, tel 0345 22 32 42, or write to MBO Solutions, Fenton Way, Laindon, Basildon, Essex SS15 6TY.

Solicitors give advice on legal problems, take action for you on your behalf and represent you in court or a tribunal (although they may engage a barrister to appear in higher courts).

There are solicitors' offices in every town and city in England and Wales. Many solicitors take legal aid cases, and some will give you a free introductory interview. However when you first make contact, it's important to ask how much the work will cost. Choosing the right firm of solicitors can be difficult. Your local CAB can give you the name of firms specialising in cases involving your particular problem.

Youth Access, 1a Taylor's Yard, 67 Alderbrook Road, London SW12 8AD, tel 0181 772 9900. If you have a problem of any kind you would like to discuss confidentially, Youth Access can put you in touch with someone locally who may be able to help. There is no charge for their service.

Life

Sex, contraception, pregnancy and abortion

British Pregnancy and Advisory Service, 7 Belgrave Road, London SW1V 1QB, tel 0171 828 2484. Information available by phone and post on contraception, pregnancy and abortion. Pregnancy testing also available.

Brook Advisory Centres, 165 Gray's Inn Road, London WC1X 8UD, tel 0171 713 9000. A free confidential service specialising in sexual and contraceptive matters for young people. Counselling also available. Cover the whole of the UK, contact the London office for details.

Family Planning Association, 2-12 Pentonville Road, London N1 9FP, runs a Contraceptive Education Helpline, Mon-Fri 9am-7pm, tel 0171 837 4044; and for Wales, **FPA Wales**, 4 Museum Place, Cardiff CF1 3BG, tel 01222 342 766 - able to give addresses of local family planning clinics and answer questions about contraception and reproductive health. There is a second office in Bangor, tel 01248 352 176.

Lesbian and Gay Switchboard, a 24 hour information and advice line, staffed by lesbian and gay volunteers, tel 0171 837 7324.

Maternity Alliance, 45 Beech Street, London EC2P 2LX. An advice line for pregnant women and new parents, open Mon - Thurs, 10am-1pm, tel 0171 588 8582. Leaflets on a wide range of issues also available, including the rights and benefits for pregnant women. Please send SAE, with an extra 1st class stamp.

Pregnancy Advisory Service, 11-13 Charlotte Street, London W1P1HD, tel 0171 637 8962. Walk-in pregnancy testing, with advice on contraception.

Stonewall, 16 Clerkenwell Close, London EC1R 0AA, tel 0171 336 8860, campaigns for equality for lesbians, gay men and bisexuals and can provide information on these issues.

HIV and AIDS

Black Liners, Unit 46, Eurolink Business Centre, 49 Effra Road London SW2 1BZ. A helpline for black people with HIV/AIDS, open Mon-Fri 10am-6pm, tel 0171 738 5274.

Body Positive, 14 Greek Street, London W1V 5LE, run a fee helpline for people who are HIV positive and their family and friends, tel 0800 616 212, open Mon-Fri, 7pm-10pm, and Sat-Sun, 4pm-10pm.

London Lighthouse, 111-117 Lancaster Road, London W11 1QT, tel 0171 792 1200. Residential, support and information centre for people affected by HIV and AIDS.

National AIDS Helpline, a 24 hour freephone service, staffed by trained counsellors who can deal with questions on sex, drugs or relationships, tel. 0800 567 123. A Welsh language service is available every day of the week between 10am-2am, tel 0800 371 131.

NAZ Project London, Palingswick House, 241 King Street, London W6 9LP, tel 0181 741 1879. Advice and support on HIV, AIDS and sexual health for people from South Asian, Middle Eastern and North African communities.

Positively Women, practical and emotional support for women with HIV and AIDS. 347-349 City Road, London EC1V 1LR, tel 0171 713 0222.

Terrence Higgins Trust, 52-54 Gray's Inn Road, London WC1X 8JU, tel 0171 831 0330. A registered charity giving information, advice and help on AIDS or HIV infection. Helpline open everyday, 12 noon - 10pm, tel 0171 242 1010. Legal advice and information is available on the Legal Line open Mon and Wed, 7pm- 9pm, tel 0171 405 2381.

Drugs and addiction

Drugaid, 34 Victoria St, Merthyr Tydfil, Mid Glamorgan, CF47 8BW, tel 01685 721991 and 64-66 Cardiff Road, Caerphilly, Mid Glamorgan, CF8 1JQ, tel 01222 881 000, offering counselling, support and information for drug and alcohol users, their friends and family.

Narcotics Anonymous, tel 0171 730 0009, a confidential helpline, open 10am- 10pm, for those trying to recover from addiction.

National Drugs Helpline, a 24 hr free confidential helpline providing advice and information on all types of drug taking for drug users, their family and friends, tel 0800 77 66 00. A Welsh language helpline is available, between 10am-2am, on 0800 371 141.

Release, 388 Old Street, London EC1V 9LT; information and legal advice service on drug-related problems, Mon-Fri, 10am-6pm, tel 0171 729 9904. Overnight helpline, tel 0171 603 8654.

SCODA (the Standing Conference on Drug Abuse), Waterbridge House, 32-36 Loman Street, London SE1 0EE, tel 0171 928 9500. Information about drug advice agencies in your area.

Health

Community Health Councils give advice to anyone who feels they have a complaint about any aspect of the health services. Under 'C' in the phone book.

MIND, Granta House, Broadway, London E15 4BQ, tel 0181 519 2122. Information on all aspects of mental health.

NHS Information Service, a free confidential service, operating normal office hours, and able to give information on a wide variety of health matters, including local contacts and what to do if you are not happy with the treatment or service you have been given, tel 0800 66 55 44.

Samaritans, will talk to anyone feeling desperate, lonely or suicidal. You can say what you like, you need not give your name, it's entirely confidential. They can be reached on the phone at any time, every day of the year. The central branch number is 0345 909090 or, for your local branch, look under 'S' in the phone book.

Sane, 1st Floor, Cityside House, 40 Adler Street, London E1 1EE, tel 0171 375 1002, able to provide information and advice to anyone (including friends and family) suffering mental health problems. They can also give callers the names of solicitors prepared to give up to a ´ hour's free advice and put them in touch with support available in their local area. A helpline operates every day of the year between 2pm-midnight, tel 0345 678 000.

Safety

Personal safety

Commission for Racial Equality, Elliott House, 10-12 Allington Street, London SW1E 5EH, tel 0171 828 7022, can give information on the law relating to racial harassment and the phone number of your local racial equality council.

Kidscape, 152 Buckingham Palace Road, London SW1W 9TR, tel 0171 730 3300, provides free information and advice on keeping safe, including bullying and how to cope with it. Send large SAE for information pack.

Rape Crisis Centres, are located throughout Britain offering to free and confidential advice to any woman or girl who has been raped or sexually assaulted. Tel 0171 837 1600, or tel. Directory Enquiries (192) for the number of your local centre.

Survivors, PO Box 2470, London SW9 9ZP, tel 0171 833 3737. Helpline open Mon-Tues, 7pm-10pm, giving advice and information to men who are victims of sexual violence.

Suzy Lamplugh Trust, 14 East Sheen Avenue, London SW14 8AS, tel 0181 392 1839. Practical information, guidance and resources on personal safety in all situations.

Victims and compensation

The Court Service publishes the Courts' Charter and other information for victims of crime, available from The Customer Service Unit, The Court Service, Southside, 105 Victoria Street, London SW1E 6QT, tel 0171 210 1775/2009/2200. Copies of the Victim's Charter are available from libraries and the Home Office, tel 0171 273 2066.

Criminal Injuries Compensation Authority, Tay House, 300 Bath Street, Glasgow, G2 4JR, tel 0141 331 2726, providing compensation for victims of crimes of violence. Write or phone for information and application forms.

Victim Support, Cranmer House, 39 Brixton Road, London SW9 6DZ, tel 0171 735 9166. There is a helpline providing support to people who have been victims of crime, Mon-Fri 9am-9pm and Sat-Sun 9am-7pm, tel 0845 30 30 900.

Education

The Advisory Centre for Education (ACE), 1b Aberdeen Studios, 22 Highbury Grove, London N5 2EA, offer telephone advice, Mon-Fri 2pm-5pm, tel 0171 354 8321 or 0171 704 9822 for calls about exclusions.

Department for Education and Employment, Public Enquiry Point, tel 0171 925 5555, able to provide information and answer questions about the law relating to education.

Independent Schools Information Service, 56 Buckingham Gate, LondonSW1E 6AG, tel 0171 630 8793, can provide information for anyone on many aspects of education for anyone who is being educated in the independent sector.

The Otherwise Club, 1 Croxley Road, London W9 3HH, tel 0181 969 0893. A community centre providing support and workshops for families choosing to educate their children out of school.

Work & Training

Commission for Racial Equality, Elliott House, 10-12 Allington Street, London SW1E 5EH, tel 0171 828 7022. Information on the all aspects of the Race Relations Acts, including employment, housing, harassment and unfair discrimination. Also able to give advice on the best way to proceed with a problem.

Department for Education and Employment, Public Enquiry Point, tel 0171 925 5555, for information on the law relating to both training & disablities.

Department of Trade and Industry, Public Enquiry Point, tel 0171 215 5000, for information on employment law.

Equal Opportunities Commission, Overseas House, Quay Street, Manchester M3 3HN; tel 0161 833 9244, and Windsor House, Windsor Lane, Cardiff CF1 3DE, tel 01222 343 552, for information on a wide range of sex discrimination and gender issues. Enquiries can be made through the Information Section, open Mon-Fri 9.30am-4.30pm.

Health and Safety Executive Information Centre, Public Enquiry Point, Broad Lane, Sheffield S3 7HQ. The Health and Safety Executive are responsible for checking health and safety at work throughout England and Wales. They can send leaflets and other information explaining the law and can tell you who to contact if you have a health and safety problem with training or at work. They also run the HSE Infoline, tel 0541 545500, open Mon-Fri 8.30am-5.00pm.

Lesbian and Gay Employment Rights (LAGER), Unit 1g, Leroy House, 436 Essex Road, London N1 3QP, advising lesbians and gay men encountering discrimination at work because of their sexuality, tel 0171 704 8066 (lesbian rights) and 0171 704 6066 (gay men).

Low Pay Unit, 27-29 Amwell Street, London EC1R 1TL, tel 0171 713 7616 can give information on the going rates of pay in particular jobs and industries and give advice on employment and benefit law. Leaflets also available, specifically written for young people. Advice line open Mon-Fri 2pm-5pm and Mon 6pm-8pm, tel 0171 713 7583.

Maternity Alliance, 45 Beech Street, London EC2P 2LX. An advice line for pregnant women and new parents open Mon - Thurs, 10am-1pm, tel 0171 588 8582. Leaflets on a wide range of issues also available, including the rights and benefits for pregnant women. Send SAE, with an extra 1st class stamp.

Money

Association of British Insurers, Consumer Information Dept., 51 Gresham Street, London EC2V 7HQ, tel 0171 600 3333, for leaflets and further information on insurance.

Benefits, for information on benefits, contact your local social security office which will be listed under Benefits Agency or Social Security in the phone book. A copy of the Benefits Agency Customer Charter is available by tel 01132 324 713. There is a free Benefit Enquiry Line for people with disabilities, tel 0800 88 22 00.

Inland Revenue, Public Enquiry Room, Room G1A, West Wing, Somerset House, The Strand, London WC2R 1LB, tel 0171 438 7772. Free leaflets and information on taxation. The Inland Revenue Self Assessment Helpline is open everyday from 8am-10pm, tel 0645 000 444.

Office of Fair Trading, Field House, 15-25 Bream's Buildings, London EC4A 1PR, tel 0171 242 2858. The official watchdog, protecting consumers' interests. They can't give advice on individual cases, but can send information on the law or put you in touch with someone who may be able to help. They have a Public Liaison Unit for general enquiries, tel 0345 22 44 99.

Trading Standards Offices, are in almost every town and city and give

CITIZENSHIP
FOUNDATION

free advice on a wide range of consumer problems. The address of your local office will be in the phone book, under 'T' or your local county or borough council.

Adoption Contact Register, Office for National Statistics, General Register Office, Adoption's Section, Trafalgar Road, Birkdale, Southport, PR8 2HH, tel 0151 471 4831. For adopted people and their birth relatives, who wish to get in touch.

Childline, Freepost 1111, London N1 OBR. Free 24 hr. helpline for any child in danger and distress, tel 0800 1111.

Kidscape, 152 Buckingham Palace Road, London SW1W 9TR, tel 0171 730 3300, provide free information and advice on keeping safe, including bullying and how to cope with it. Send large SAE for information pack.

Law Society Children Panel, The Law Society, Ipsley Court, Berrington Close, Redditch, Worcestershire B98 0TD, tel 01527 517 141, can put you in touch with a local solicitor who can advise and represent you in matters concerning parental and other family relationships.

Message Home Helpline, a confidential service allowing someone who has run away from home to leave a message for family and friends to let them know they are alive and well, tel (free) 0800 700740.

National Council for One-Parent Families, 255 Kentish Town Road, London NW5 2LX, tel 0171 267 1361, provides free information booklets for lone parents on many subjects including benefits, tax, legal rights and divorce.

National Missing Persons Charity provides a helpline giving help, information and advice to families of missing people. Roebuck House, 284-286 Upper Richmond Road West, East Sheen, London SW14 7JE, tel (free) 0500 700700.

National Society for the Prevention of Cruelty to Children (NSPCC), National Centre, 42 Curtain Road, London EC2A 3NH, tel 0171 825 2500. The NSPCC runs a free 24 hr child protection helpline for children and young people, parents and other adults, tel 0800 800 500.

NORCAP (National Organisation for the Counselling of Adoptees and Parents), 112 Church Road, Wheatley, Oxfordshire OX33 1LU, tel 01865 875 000, provides advice and practical support for adopted people and their birth relatives who wish to get in touch. Open Mon-Thurs 10am-4pm and Fri 10am-12noon.

Stepfamily, Chapel House, 18 Hatton Place, London, EC1N 8RU, tel 0171 209 2460, gives information and advice to any member of a stepfamily or anyone affected by stepfamilies.

Women's Aid gives information, support and advice for women experiencing domestic violence in the home. **Women's Aid England** run a helpline, Mon-Thurs 10am-5pm and Fri 10am- 3pm, tel 0345 023 468. **Welsh Women's Aid** is open Mon-Fri 10am-3pm, tel 01222 390 874 (Cardiff), 01970 612 748 (Aberystwyth), 01745 334767 (Rhyl).

Home

Black Liners, Unit 46, Eurolink Business Centre, 49 Effra Road London SW2 1BZ, tel 0171 738 7468. Counselling, housing advice and drop-in centre for black people.

Campaign for Bedsit Rights, 20 Club Row, London E2 7EY, tel 0171 739 8877, advice and information on a wide range of issues, including safety, security of tenure and repairs.

Centrepoint, Bewlay House, 2 Swallow Place, London W1R 7AA, tel 0171 544 5000, can advise callers who have arrived in London with nowhere to stay.

Shelter, 88 Old Street, London EC1V 9HU, tel 0171 505 2000. Information on all aspects of housing rights. Shelter also run a 24 hour emergency service for homeless people in London, tel 0800 446 441.

Leisure

Centre for Accessible Environments, Nutmeg House, 60 Gainsford Street, London SE1 2NY, tel 0171 357 8182, for advice and information on deaing with problems of access to buildings.

Countryside Commission, John Dower House, Crescent Place, Cheltenham, Gloucestershire GL50 3RA, tel 01242 521 381, for information on access and rights of way.

Department of the Environment, Transport and the Regions has a Public Enquiry Point, giving information on a wide range of environmental issues, open Mon-Fri 9am-5pm, tel 0171 890 3333.

Environment Agency, Rio House, Waterside Drive, Aztec West, Almonds-bury, Bristol BS32 4UD, tel 01454 624 400, runs a free 24 hour phone line on which you can report any environmental incident, tel 0800 80 70 60.

Proof of Age Card Scheme, The Portman Group, 2d Wimpole Street, London W1M 7AA, tel 0171 499 1010.

If you're 18 or over and have trouble in proving your age, you can get a Proof of Age Card from the Portman Group, an organisation set up by the drinks industry against alcohol misuse.

Royal Society for the Prevention of Cruelty to Animals (RSPCA) have a 24 hour emergency line for people who wish to report an animal in distress, tel 0990 555 999. For other information contact The RSPCA Public Enquiry Section, Causeway, Horsham, West Sussex, RH12 1HG, tel 01403 264 181.

Travel & Transport

ABTA (The Association of British Travel Agents), 68-71 Newman Street, London W1P 4AH, have an information line dealing with general advice on ABTA, its members and other travel information, tel 0891 202 520 (calls charged at 49.5p per minute) all other enquiries, tel 0171 637 2444.

Department of the Environment, Transport and the Regions has a Public Enquiry Point, for enquiries on motoring and transport law, open Mon-Fri 9am-5pm, tel 0171 890 3333.

Driving Standards Agency, Stanley House, 56 Talbot Street, Nottingham NG1 5GU, tel 01159 012 500, for information on motorcycle licences and training.

DVLA, Licensing Centre, Swansea, SA6 7JL, for enquiries over driving licences, tax discs or the registration details of a particular vehicle, tel 01792 772 151.

National Express Ltd., Ensign Court, 4 Vicarage Road, Edgbaston, Birmingham, B15 3ES, tel 0121 625 1122. Information on coach travel and discount travel schemes. For telephone bookings call 0990 808080, open every day 8am-10pm.

Royal Society for the Prevention of Accidents (RoSPA), Edgbaston Park, 353 Bristol Road, Birmingham, B5 7ST, tel 0121 248 2000. Information on safety on the road (and home). For a quicker reply, enclose a SAE.

Police & Courts

Citizens Advice Bureau (CAB) have trained staff who can give free legal advice and suggest solicitors able to deal with your particular problem. See **General** section, above, for more details.

The Court Service publishes the *Courts' Charter* explaining how the court system works and what you can expect if you are charged with a criminal offence or attend court as a witness, a member of a jury or as a defendant or plaintiff in a civil case. The Charter is available from The Customer Service Unit, The Court Service, Southside, 105 Victoria Street, London SW1E 6QT, tel 0171 210 1775/2009/2200.

Duty Solicitor Scheme provides anyone who is questioned by the police about an offence with free legal advice, any time of day or night. You may ask for a solicitor you know, or you can choose from a list kept by the police.

Legal Aid Board, head office, 85 Gray's Inn Road, London WC1X 8AA, tel 0171 813 1000. Information leaflets available on applying for legal aid.

Police Complaints Authority, 10 Great George Street, London SW1P 3AE, tel 0171 273 6450. The official body overseeing complaints against the police, which can provide information on how to make a

complaint if you have witnessed or suffered police misconduct.

Law & Government

Information
European Commission, 8 Storey's Gate, Westminster, London SW1P 3AT, tel 0171 973 1992. Explanatory leaflets available. If you phone, ask for the Information Section.

European Parliament Information Office, 2 Queen Anne's Gate, London SW1H 9AA, tel 0171 227 4300. An information service on all matters relating to the European Parliament.

House of Commons Information Office, House of Commons, London SW1A 2TT, tel 0171 219 4272. A public information service on the working and proceedings of Parliament.

Service First, for a list of national charters call the Service First publications line, tel 0345 22 32 42, or write to MBO Solutions, Fenton Way, Laindon, Basildon, Essex SS15 6TY. If you would like to nominate a public service for a Charter Mark, write to Charter Mark Nominations, Room 65B/G, Cabinet Office, Horse Guards Road, London SW1P 3AL, tel 0645 400 444.

Political parties
Conservative Party, tel 0171 222 9000.

Green Party, tel 0171 272 4474.

Labour Party, tel 0171 802 1000.

Liberal Democrats, tel 0171 222 7999.

Plaid Cymru, the Party of Wales, tel 01222 646 000.

A

Abortion 7
Abusive phone calls 22
Accommodation
- agencies 70
- council housing 73
- deposits 70
- eviction 72-5
- finding 70
- lodgings 73
- repairs 74
- service charge 70-1
- tenancy agreement 72-3
Adoption 6-7, 63
Age
- of consent 4-5
- of criminal responsibility 110
- proof of 79
AIDS 8-9, 11
Alcohol 13, 78-9, 83, 85, 99
Animals 88
Assault 19, 81
- indecent 5, 21
- in marriage 68, 113

B

Baby-sitting 63
Bail 107
Banks 55, 91
Beaches 87
Bigamy 65
Blood donors 16
Bouncers 81
Bulls 86
Burglary 19
Bus travel 92-3

C

Charter Mark 118
Charters
- Benefit Agency 58
- Courts' 19
- Jobseeker's 37
- Mental Health Services 16
- Patient's 16
- Redundancy Payments Service 46
- Train Operators' 93
- Victims 19

Cheque guarantee card 55
Citizen's arrest 18
Citizenship 61
Coach travel 92-3
Compensation - criminal injuries 18-21
Consumer law 48-57, 78-9, 90-1, 96-7
Contraception 6
Contract
- consumer 48-51, 78, 90, 93
- at work 34, 38, 43-4
Copyright 84
Corporal punishment 27, 62, 114
Courts 112-3
- Crown 110
- magistrate's 108, 110
- small claims 51
- youth 110
Crash helmets 99
Credit 52-4
Credit cards 52-3, 90
Crime
- reporting to the police 18
Crown Prosecution Service 108
Customs 92
Cycling 97

D

Dentists 14-5
Discrimination
- disability 37, 45, 78, 80, 82
- housing 75
- racial 36, 41-2, 45, 75, 78, 80
- sex 36, 41-2, 45, 75, 78, 80, 113
- work 9, 41-2, 45
Divorce 65-7
Doctors
- confidentiality 6, 8, 13
- registering and changing 13-4
Drugs
- illegal 10-2, 80, 83
- police powers 12, 80
Duty solicitor

E

Elections 115-6
Electoral Register 115
Engagements 65
European
- Convention on Human Rights 114
- Law 113, 116
- Parliament 113, 116
Eviction 74-5

F

Fingerprints 106
Fireworks 81
Fishing 86
Footpaths 86

G

Gambling 81
Gay relationships 5, 36-7
Glue sniffing 13
Grandparents 68

H

Harassment 20
- by landlord 74-5
- racial 20-1
- sexual 42
Hire purchase 53
HIV 8-9, 11
Holidays 90-2
Homelessness 76
Housing benefit 71
Hunt saboteurs 118

I

Industrial action 44
Industrial tribunals 35, 39, 41-2, 45-6
Insurance 56-7
- household 75, 83
- motor vehicle 82, 92, 95, 100
- travel 90-1
Interest rates 52, 54

J

Judicial review 118
Juries 109-10

K

Knives 22

USE THE LAW WITH CARE. TRY TALKING FIRST.